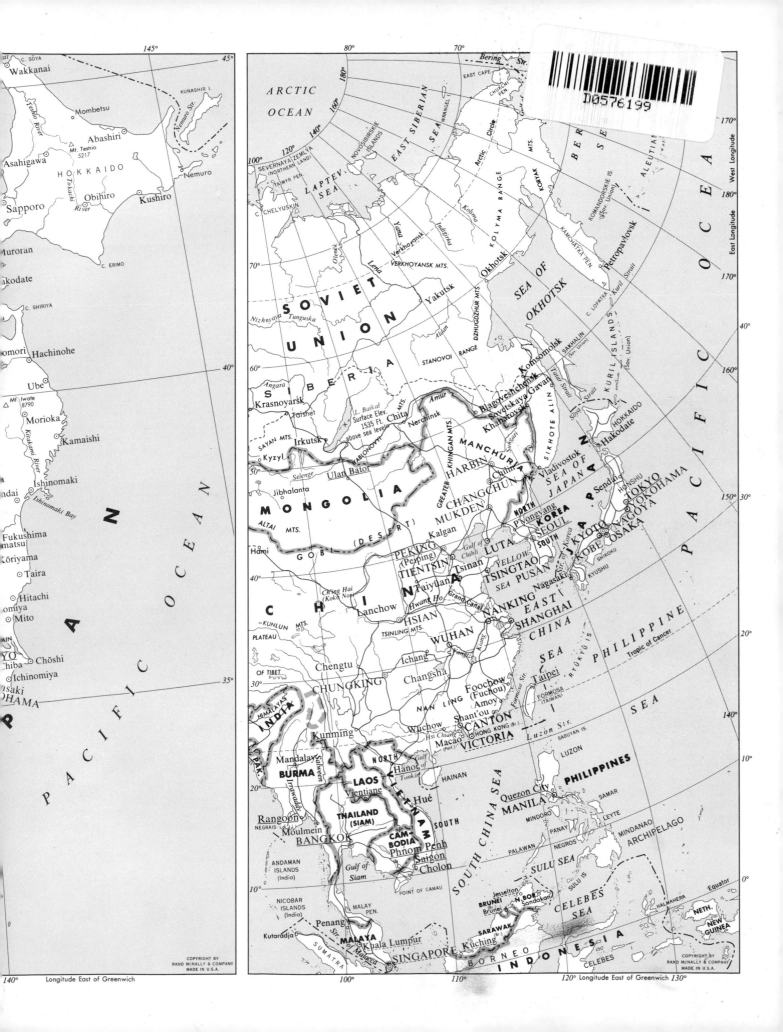

LIFE WORLD LIBRARY

JAPAN

OTHER BOOKS BY THE EDITORS OF LIFE:

LIFE's Picture History of World War II

LIFE's Picture History of Western Man

The World We Live In
with Lincoln Barnett

The World's Great Religions

America's Arts and Skills

Picture Cook Book

The Second World War
with Winston S. Churchill

The Wonders of Life on Earth
with Lincoln Barnett

LIFE Pictorial Atlas of the World
with the Editors of Rand McNally

LIFE WORLD LIBRARY

JAPAN

by Edward Seidensticker

and The Editors of LIFE

TIME INCORPORATED · NEW YORK · 1961

ABOUT THE WRITER

In the text of this volume, Edward Seidensticker gives an interpretation of Japan based on more than 13 years of residence in the country, where he has won a reputation as a sensitive interpreter of the Japanese people and an incisive commentator on the contemporary scene. His knowledge of the country dates from 1945, when he served for a time as a Marine officer with the U.S. Occupation Forces. Mr. Seidensticker, who was born in Colorado, returned to Tokyo in 1948 for two years' service with the Department of State and then did graduate work at the University of Tokyo, where he later taught courses in Japanese cultural history. A noted translator of classical and modern Japanese literature, he also writes a newspaper column called "This Country" for the English-language edition of *Yomiuri* in Tokyo, and contributes to general and scholarly publications in the United States and Europe.

Contents

		Page
	Introduction	7
Chapter 1	The Crowded Country	9
Chapter 2	The Heritage of a Long Isolation	25
Chapter 3	Storm and Calm in Politics	43
Chapter 4	A Resilient and Growing Economy	61
Chapter 5	Upheavals in Family and Society	77
Chapter 6	Traces of Spirit	89
Chapter 7	Diversions Borrowed and Preserved	105
Chapter 8	The Tolerant Believers	119
Chapter 9	Powerful Molders of Young Minds	133
Chapter 10	A Nation in the Balance	145
	Appendix	152
	Credits	156
	Index	157

COVER: Visitors walk the rain-washed courtyards of Tōshōgū Shrine in Nikkō

TIME INC. BOOK DIVISION

Editor
NORMAN P. ROSS

Copy Director *Art Director*
WILLIAM JAY GOLD LEONARD JOSSEL

Chief of Research
BEATRICE T. DOBIE

"Japan" was produced by the following editorial staff:

Editor, LIFE World Library OLIVER E. ALLEN

Designer BEN SCHULTZ

Chief Researcher GRACE BRYNOLSON

Researchers IRENE S. ERTUGRUL, JEAN SULZBERGER
PATRICIA APPEL

Picture Researchers MARGARET K. GOLDSMITH
JOAN T. LYNCH

Art Associates ALBERT J. DUNN, ROBERT L. YOUNG

Art Assistants JAMES D. SMITH, RICHARD FORTE
JOHN M. WOODS

Copy Staff MARIAN GORDON GOLDMAN
REBECCA CHAITIN, DOLORES A. LITTLES
MARGARET RAMSAY, ESTHER KAPLAN

•

Publisher JEROME S. HARDY

General Manager JOHN A. WATTERS

•

LIFE MAGAZINE

Managing Editor *Publisher*
EDWARD K. THOMPSON C. D. JACKSON

•

The text for the chapters of this book was written by Edward Seidensticker, for the picture essays by Jack Winocour. The following individuals and departments of LIFE Magazine were instrumental in producing the book: Margaret Bourke-White, John Dominis, Eliot Elisofon, J. R. Eyerman and Howard Sochurek, staff photographers; Don Connery and other members of the Tokyo Bureau; Gene Farmer, Foreign News Editor; Ray Mackland, Picture Editor; George Caturani, Chief of the Foreign News Bureau; Doris O'Neil, Chief of the LIFE Picture Library; and Content Peckham, Chief of the Time Inc. Bureau of Editorial Reference. Special assistance and advice were also provided by Charles Elliott and Frank Gibney of LIFE.

Introduction

In 1852, when Commodore Perry sailed for Japan, his instructions pointed out that recent events had brought America and the nations of the East close together, that intercourse between them had increased and "no limits can be assigned to its future extension." Today we know this is true.

Japan's role in the future development of Asia is of crucial importance. It is so recognized by the Russians and the Chinese Communists, who, as noted in a Rockefeller Brothers Fund report, have set "a high priority on undermining Japan's present position and ultimately obtaining its adherence to the Communist camp."

For Americans it is vitally important to have a knowledge and understanding of the 90 million vigorous, confused and complicated people of Japan. This remarkable book by Edward Seidensticker and the Editors of LIFE, with its accompanying illustrations, goes further toward meeting this need than anything else I have seen.

Here we learn how the moral code of the Tokugawa shoguns—who kept Japan in isolation for some two hundred years—with its emphasis on loyalty of inferior to superior, has molded modern Japan.

We learn of the restless Japan of today, of a people who, as a result of the destruction by the war of many of their old traditions, feel they belong to nothing at all. We learn of a people who love baseball and yet cherish a ritualistic form of wrestling called *sumō* whose origins reach into antiquity. And we are introduced to the wonderful world of Japanese art and what it means to the people today.

To those who are worried about what role Japan will play in the free world's struggle with Communist imperialism, this book has much to offer. We learn how a well-meaning Occupation reform of Japan's educational system has contributed to the ideological confusion of Japan's youth, and how an American-inspired Constitution has contributed to Japan's reluctance to assume the obligations of her own defense.

I particularly commend to American readers the final chapter of Mr. Seidensticker's text, with its wise advice concerning what we should do if we are to have any influence on Japan's future course. As he says, we should be quiet, be strong and, above all, be patient.

JOHN M. ALLISON
former U.S. Ambassador to Japan

Jostling crowds throng the sidewalk of a street in Tokyo's Shinjuku district, a popular shopping and entertainment area. Scenes like

8

this one are typical of a city bursting at the seams with people

1

The Crowded Country

IF a visitor to Tokyo comes in across the Pacific at night, he will be aware of a sudden blaze of light, a cosmic explosion on the edge of a vast darkness. If he comes in by day, he will see below him, through the industrial smoke, a huge expanse of gray and brown, remarkable for its want of greenery and its dearth of striking features, save for a few towers that bespeak the importance of electronics in modern Japan.

Once through customs he will plunge into the struggle to reach the heart of the city. As he edges nearer, through what seems an immovable mass of vehicles, his impression will be of people—a wall of people. A population of 14.2 million makes the Tokyo metropolitan area the world's second biggest (New York is first).

When he has learned to look above the people in downtown Tokyo, his impression may well be of what a well-known British writer not long ago called "a tortured use of space." Tokyo is not a beautiful city. It has one good walk leading around the moat of the Imperial Palace, with its gray-green stone embankments and grassy slopes surmounted by fine (but on close inspection soot-covered) trees. But beyond that, Tokyo is a jumble of signs and inadequate streets and undistinguished buildings. It has neither the harmonious horizontal lines of a European city nor the striking vertical ones of an American city. The newcomer must bring his eye down again to the wall of people, for in their vitality lies the charm of the city.

But suppose the visitor comes not across the Pacific from the east but from the Asiatic mainland west of Japan. Suppose he is a Korean. For purposes of collecting strong impressions he will be well advised to fly over Japan in the late afternoon and land in Tokyo at nightfall. The country below him in the late afternoon sun will seem astonishingly green, because the Japanese are remarkable among the peoples of eastern Asia for having kept their trees. Korea has a wasted, harsh, hibernal look. Its mountains are bare and visibly sliding into the rivers. In Japan the mountains are covered.

When the visiting Korean arrives in Tokyo in the gathering darkness, he will be impressed not by the masses of bodies (for Seoul is a city of two million built for perhaps a third of that number) nor by the clutter and lack of distinction in the city's façade (for modern Seoul, too,

was built by the Japanese). Instead he will be immediately aware that Japan is far from the poorest country in the world. He will be awed by the extravagant use of electricity. To the traveler from dark Seoul or from the still darker Korean countryside, any city that can turn on so many lights all at once seems especially fat and rich. In 1960 South Korea sent a "friendship delegation" of students to Japan, and they spent much of their time just sitting with their mouths open, watching the lights.

Tokyo is many things, but above all it is a roiling mass of humanity, and an appalling jam. A study published in 1959 established that there were more neon lights in Tokyo than any other city in the world, and more movie theaters. As for noise, it was estimated that Tokyo produced in 10 seconds the same amount of honking that New York took a full hour to accumulate. Figuring on an ideally smooth flow of traffic, the police should allow no more than 35,000 vehicles to pass Iwaitabashi, the busiest intersection in Tokyo, during any 12-hour period; but one day a few years ago almost 100,000 were counted between 7 a.m. and 7 p.m.

This was in 1956. Late in 1960 the Metropolitan Police announced that on an average day there were six major traffic jams in Tokyo, and, with the number of vehicles increasing at a rate of 10,000 every month, there were still more

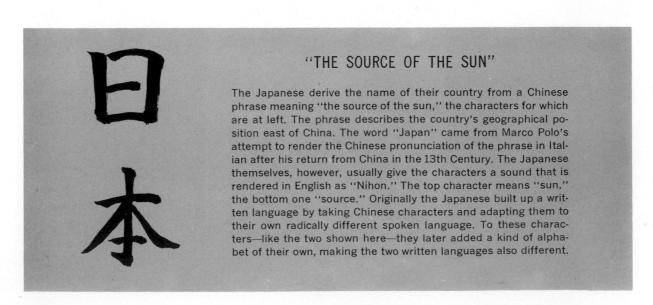

"THE SOURCE OF THE SUN"

The Japanese derive the name of their country from a Chinese phrase meaning "the source of the sun," the characters for which are at left. The phrase describes the country's geographical position east of China. The word "Japan" came from Marco Polo's attempt to render the Chinese pronunciation of the phrase in Italian after his return from China in the 13th Century. The Japanese themselves, however, usually give the characters a sound that is rendered in English as "Nihon." The top character means "sun," the bottom one "source." Originally the Japanese built up a written language by taking Chinese characters and adapting them to their own radically different spoken language. To these characters—like the two shown here—they later added a kind of alphabet of their own, making the two written languages also different.

in prospect for 1961. One day recently traffic stalled for two and a half hours before the Imperial Palace, moved for a half hour, and stalled again for an hour and a half; and on the same day traffic was stalled for two hours in another part of the city. Osaka holds the national traffic jam record, however. One day in 1960 traffic was stalled before Osaka Station for 10 hours, in the course of which most of the taxis in the city ran out of gas.

DESPITE the crush, however, there are still not enough vehicles to fill the demand. Day by day it becomes more difficult to find a taxi, and on a rainy day it is usually quicker to walk. The trains are full, too. The National Railways announced late in 1960 that a certain section of the downtown Tokyo Loop Line was carrying three times its capacity during the rush hour, and that the line to the western suburbs was operating at two and a half times capacity. Sometimes it seems even traffic on foot must stop. On almost every evening Tokyo's main shopping section, the Ginza, is as crowded as Times Square is on New Year's Eve, and on Christmas Eve—the night that is to Tokyo what New Year's Eve is to New York—the Ginza regularly holds close to a million people.

The pressure on the land is enormous. As the city spreads farther into the farmlands around it, commuters must travel farther and farther (some spend five and six hours a day going back and forth). The person with property near the center of Tokyo can sit back and wait for his land to double in value every two or three years, and the renter has no recourse but to pay more and more. Toward the end of 1960 the Tokyo Real Estate Association announced that property in and near the Ginza had doubled in value since 1958. In the same two-year period the value of land in a fashionable residential district to the southwest almost quintupled. In other big cities matters are little better, although Kyoto still manages to occupy its river banks with quiet dignity. Kyoto, however, has another kind of problem: the swarms of people grimly pursuing a great national pastime, travel.

If crowding is an essential fact about Japan, other important facts must also be noted—meteorological and geographical facts. The Japanese archipelago—four main islands and several hundred smaller ones—lies within the range of the monsoon winds of southern and eastern Asia. Geologically Japan is very new. It is a green country, and a country of mountains and rivers. Even in the middle of the largest plain in Japan one is never out of sight of a mountain. The traveler on the seven-hour rail journey from Tokyo to Kobe traverses the three great plains of Japan; but he has left the Kanto Plain at the head of Tokyo Bay even before he is out of Yokohama, has come to the outskirts of the Nagoya metropolitan complex before he is far out on the Nobi Plain, and has found mountains closing off the Kinki Plain by the time he has left Osaka.

It is only a slight exaggeration to say that any terrain open enough to allow the eye a wide, continued view is occupied by an enormous concentration of people, so that there may be no view at all. Along the way, to be sure, our traveler has been treated to one of the grand vistas of Japan: the unbroken sweep from the shores of Suruga Bay to the top of Mount Fuji. Most of the time, however, he has seen little but narrow valleys shut off by mountains or perhaps by mountains and the sea.

ALTHOUGH Japan is a very beautiful country, it has surprisingly little variety. A trip to one of its celebrated scenic spots is likely to prove a disappointment, for the dutiful pilgrim will have seen much on his journey there that is just as beautiful, and beautiful in much the same way. The typical view would include a valley floor that is an intricate patchwork of velvet, under water much of the year, changing with the rice cycle from a delicate yellow-green in the spring and early summer to the emerald of midsummer, then to green-gold and to brown, and, when the cycle is over, striped with the darker green of the winter crops. The patchwork would continue up the terraced hills. There would be a small river, and perhaps a lake or reservoir; a village in the shadow of a hill, the brown-black harmony of its tile and thatched roofs broken by an ungainly schoolhouse and a maze of wires, showing that Japan is a land of universal education and rural electrification; a complexity of greens on the slopes of the uncultivated hills, from a feathery touch of bamboo that is the color of the rice paddies at planting time, through the darker, waxy green of persimmon and camellia, to the near black of the shrine-grove cedars. If the valley opens on the sea, the village may look out over a silver-blue inlet, a scattering of pine-topped islands, the floats of fishing nets in an arrangement of ellipses, and perhaps beds of cultivated seaweed, a diaphanous veil of green at low tide surmounted by a golden haze of bamboo poles, a marvel of functional beauty.

IT is a landscape of soft tones and of a soft, misty air, the reverse of the hard, bright contrasts of Mediterranean Europe. There may be abrupt seasonal colors, a blossoming cherry or plum or wild camellia, and there may be a vermilion shrine gate; but, on the whole, sudden colors come as an intrusion. They are furnished by billboards selling modern gadgets, or by foreign horticulture, which the rural housewife often prefers to the native art. In the summer the farmyard is likely to be garnished with a patch of cerise and orange zinnias, and in the autumn the ubiquitous flower is the cosmos, which reminds the Japanese of the cherry blossom and blooms much longer.

The monsoons bring heavy and predictable seasonal moisture, which encourages rice culture. In the late spring and early summer, moist, warm winds and steady rains come in from the Pacific, keeping the stems of the newly transplanted rice seedlings under water. In the winter the cold and dry winds from Siberia pick up moisture over the Sea of Japan, giving the northwest coast of the largest island the heaviest snowfall in the world for its latitudes and altitudes. Tokyo and the heavily populated Pacific side have fluctuating precipitation rates which on a graph would show up as two valleys (the hot, muggy but relatively clear summers and

the bright, cold winters) lying between peaks (the rains of the planting season and those of the harvest season). The last are often disastrous, because they come in on the violent tropical storms known as typhoons.

Japan's geological situation brings further natural unpleasantness. In a period so recent that, as one geographer has put it, "there has not been time to round off the edges," the Japanese islands were pushed up from the ocean by crustal folding and volcanic eruption. They thus form a part of the line of new, rugged mountains that fringe the Pacific from Cape Horn up through Alaska and southwest to New Zealand. The line is one of earthquakes, and nowhere on it, except possibly in the East Indies, is the seismic threat more persistent than it is in Japan. The Japanese earth is constantly trembling. Japanese seismographs record 20 noteworthy shocks on an average day, most of them in well-defined zones. Osaka lies in one, and the heart of the Fuji zone is near enough to Tokyo to devastate that city from time to time. Tokyo was wrecked in 1855 and, together with Yokohama, again in 1923.

Japan must be described as a land of natural disasters—typhoons, earthquakes, floods and fires (which often accompany earthquakes). Yet the Japanese are astonishingly unafraid of nature, and they often show a loving awareness of delicate seasonal changes. The forces that have made Japan a land of natural violence have also made it a land of natural loveliness.

PASSING through a typical landscape, one may find much to disturb the ear—a loudspeaker, perhaps, selling apples or urging the cause of a candidate for office or simply playing popular music. But to the eye the scene is a quiet one. In spite of the population statistics, the countryside can on occasion even seem lonely. Japan's crowding is not uniform, and the pull of the cities is enormous. Sometimes, as the train stops at a provincial station in the autumn dusk, there seems to be a feeling of sadness in the air. Most of the people off in the little clusters of lights would far rather be in the train heading back to the city. The waitress at the loveliest resort can be expected to talk longingly of Tokyo, and ask to be put in one's baggage.

Japan is not as small as the Japanese like to think it is. Although it is only a twentieth the size of the United States, it is half again as large as the United Kingdom, and about the size of East and West Germany together. The four main islands stretch for about 1,300 miles in an arc northeast to southwest, at latitudes corresponding to those of the American Atlantic Coast from Georgia north. It takes about 20 hours to reach the far southwest from Tokyo by crack express, and almost twice that time by train and boat to the far northeast.

IF Japan is not the tiny little garden patch of a country we are told it is, however, it is still extremely crowded. The 1960 census showed the population to be 93.4 million, or well over half that of the United States—and on less than a twentieth of the soil. The average population density, about 654 people per square mile, is slightly lower than that of the Netherlands and Belgium, but since less than a seventh of the land is cultivated, as against about a third for the Netherlands and Belgium (both of which also have far richer pasture and meadow lands), the population per unit of productive land is the highest in the world. Even in overcrowded Asia, only Formosa, South Korea and Java—all of them fractions of countries—are serious rivals in this regard. Japan is the fifth most populous country in the world, coming after China, India, the U.S.S.R. and the United States.

Yet here emerges a puzzle: one cannot be completely sure whether Japan is overpopulated or not. Between 1955 and 1960 the population increased by four million people. Although the birth rate is falling sharply—in the 10 years from 1947 to 1957 it was cut in half, dropping to about the level of West Germany and Switzerland—the Japanese Ministry of Welfare predicts that the population will level off only toward the end of this century. The hundred-million mark will have been passed by about 1970, and in 1975 the population will still be growing by more than half a million per year.

Even while the Ministry of Welfare puts out these figures, however, the Economic Planning Board predicts that Japan in the not distant future will have a shortage of labor. Furthermore, the population growth is taking place mainly in the cities. The farm population has fallen by almost a tenth in the last decade, and it is now down to slightly more than a third of the country's total. While more than half of the 46 prefectures in Japan were losing people between 1955 and 1960, the major population centers—Tokyo-Yokohama, Nagoya, Osaka-Kobe-Kyoto, and North Kyushu—were gaining more than the total gain for the country. The single prefecture of Tokyo registered almost a third of the national gain, and the two prefectures of Tokyo and Osaka more than half.

Another essential fact about Japan is almost too obvious to need stating: its insularity. Although Japan is frequently compared to another island country off the opposite shore of the Eurasian land mass, it is far more remotely insular than England. The Strait of Korea—110 miles across—is a good four times as wide as the Strait of Dover.

CROSSING the Strait of Korea today is a simple matter. But in centuries past when a literate Japanese culture was being put together under Chinese influence, the geographical barrier was a formidable one. Any Japanese trader or diplomat trying to reach the center of the East Asian world was confronted by a very perilous journey. First came the difficult crossing of the strait. Once across, he was at the remote tip of the Korean peninsula, which was itself on the remote outer edges of the Chinese cultural sphere, and to reach the Chinese capital he had either to sail around Korea or take his chances on the open sea. At the end of the journey he was confronted by a Chinese court that would have thought the notion of intercourse as equals unspeakably grotesque.

Over the centuries, Japan borrowed much from Chinese culture, and China borrowed relatively little in return. Through most of their history the Japanese were left alone to develop their own culture; they were far more interested in foreigners than most foreigners were in them. In modern times their insularity has been preserved by a stubborn language barrier. Japanese is an orphan language complicated by what is probably the most irrational system of writing that was ever invented.

The fact of insularity helps explain the Japanese when they seem most puzzling. The Tokyo taxi driver will chat about the state of the city and the world, will suddenly remark amiably that he does not much like foreigners—and then will proceed to ask the visitor for *his* views about the city and the world. The young lady in one of the "singing tearooms" where leftist students gather goes on singing the latest defiant "peace" song from Moscow, even while she pours for the visitor:

You may not drop the atom bomb!
No, not through my skies!

Yet this young lady would be the most surprised person in the world if she were told that her strong declaration might seem unnecessarily challenging. Both taxi driver and young lady are untroubled by what their acts imply, and this casualness derives at least in part from the insular Japanese tradition of importing finished moral and religious systems from abroad. With the tradition has grown up a tolerance of contradiction; in the past a man found nothing very strange about calling himself a Confucian-Buddhist, and today he may just as easily call himself a Christian-Communist.

PHYSICALLY the Japanese may be described as a homogeneous people closely related to the nearest peoples on the continent. That they came in successive waves of immigration from the continent seems to be an established fact, although their ultimate origins are obscure. The Japanese commonly believe that they can spot a Korean (whom they look down upon), but most Japanese, fully clothed, are indistinguishable from most Koreans. Bereft of their clothes, they are frequently to be distinguished by a tendency toward hairiness, revealing mixture with a people distant from the Koreans (one such people, the Ainu of northern Japan, survives precariously).

The great British student of Japan, Basil Hall Chamberlain, offered this description of the Japanese half a century ago: "Compared with people of European race, the average Japanese has a long body and short legs, a large skull with a tendency to prognathism (projecting jaws), a flat nose, coarse hair, scanty eye-lashes, puffy eyelids, a sallow complexion, and a low stature." Except perhaps for the sallowness and the shortness, which improved nutrition is now changing, this is still true today, and it is not a pleasant picture. Yet in actual life the details add up to a face that is sometimes very good-looking, and frequently likable and engaging. Though not as given to laughter as the Koreans and Chinese, the Japanese are likely to impress one as a sunny people. The Japanese smile is a complex one, possibly containing sadness and uncertainty, but its pleasantness is still enough to obscure the frequently bad teeth. It was this pleasant look, perhaps, that made the historian Sir George Sansom argue that there is "a warm, southern element in their composition."

THEY are a most industrious people. Only constant toil has made it possible for the Japanese farmer to produce yields per unit of land that are among the highest in the world. The Japanese are also noted for being clean and tidy, although this characteristic has its limits. The institution of the bath not only as something useful but as something pleasant does a great deal to make life at close Tokyo quarters bearable. When it comes to keeping their surroundings tidy, however, the matter is more complex. It is often said that the Japanese are scrupulously tidy at home and frenzied scatterers of litter when away from home. The visual evidence certainly supports the second half of the statement. The litter after a cherry-viewing party or a May Day rally is something like the aftermath of an explosion.

In an office, the messiness is perhaps the chief argument against the modern, glassed-in building. The building itself may not be untidy, but one's admiration quickly gives way to horrified fascination at the clutter of desks and tissue paper and teapots and drying linen within.

The interiors of Japanese houses are known as models of clean simplicity, but they are often clean only where the visitor is likely to look. One does well not to raise an eye or a finger to a door lintel, and the beams of a hundred-year-old farm cottage may be festooned with cobwebs also a hundred years old. The wooden verandas of that same farm cottage, on the other hand, will have been washed, perhaps repeatedly, every day of those hundred years.

It is often said that the Japanese are a very polite people, and it is undeniable that they are much given to ceremony. But it might also be said that they are extremely ceremonious toward those whom they know, and highly unceremonious toward others. Few urban Japanese bother to say "Excuse me" after stepping on a person's toe or knocking a book out of his hand—provided the person is a stranger. If he is known, it is common to apologize for offenses that have not been committed. "I behaved very badly the other day," is a common greeting from one friend to another, even though only pleasantries were exchanged the other day. An American once caught the essence of the matter in an uncaptioned cartoon. Two Japanese were industriously bowing to each other in a revolving door, holding up lines of people on either side.

As a people the Japanese are good with their hands. They excel at handicrafts and are per-

HOW JAPANESE IS PRONOUNCED

Japanese vowels are pronounced as in Italian, consonants as in English (except that "g" is always hard). For most purposes it is best to give each syllable the same weight. A long mark over a vowel means not that it should be accented, but that it should be pronounced twice as long as it usually is, as if it occurred two times in a row. The pronunciation of various words found in this book is shown below.

Fujiwara: Foo·jee·wah·rah
Minamoto: Mee·nah·mo·to
Genji: Ghen·jee
Ise: Ee·seh
Sumō: Soo·mo·o
Geisha: Gay·sha
Haiku: High·ku

haps the world's supreme potters and workers of wood. Along with the dexterity and eagerness to learn from others goes the famous capacity for imitation. There can be no question that it exists, and that because of it the Japanese are able to economize on research. A German company will spend years developing a safety release to keep a skier from breaking his leg, and that winter a native product, identical to all the decorations, will show up on Japanese slopes. Yet two points ought to be made to challenge the notion that the Japanese are only copiers and pirates. The first is that they frequently go ahead on their own to make original contributions. Half a century ago, visitors from Europe often complained about the poor quality of Japanese fruit. Today there are few peoples in the world to rival the Japanese at producing a strawberry or a peach. Their cameras and transistor radios are also remarkable.

The second point is that things change when they come to Japan. Though gadgets like a ski release may be exceptions, most things, from a flush toilet to a method of art reproduction, take on a distinctly Japanese air upon arrival. A neon sign can become a marvel of subtle color modulation; Confucianism in Japan quietly drops its Chinese metaphysics. There is a novel by Tanizaki in which a young man has an excessive fondness for western things but his own way of arranging them. To save steps, he has his bathtub in the living room along with everything else.

It is something of a puzzle that a nation so well organized when it comes to producing transistor radios would be so badly organized in other ways. Sometimes, as in 1960, when mobs rioted against the Japanese alliance with the U.S. but seemed to offer no very realistic alternative, Japan impresses the observer as having not the faintest idea of what it is and what it is up to. Unfortunately, contemporary ideology has not kept pace with contemporary technology. In view of the Japanese ability for more than a millennium to make pretty and clever things, and their indifference, through that same millennium, toward rational or creative speculation, it is not surprising that such should be the case. Just as some of the things done by the Japanese in the name of Confucianism today would have seemed strange and irrational to the Chinese a few centuries ago, so some of the things that Japan does in the name of democracy seem strange and irrational today to Westerners.

PERHAPS the Japanese are best revealed through an examination of their social relationships, although here an element of speculation must enter. It may be immediately apparent that they come in crowds; it is less apparent —but also true—that they cling together like some frightened, beleaguered tribe even when they have room to spread out. The stories one reads of families of seven and eight members living in one room are less horrifying than they would be if one did not suspect, from the behavior of families with many rooms, that they would not have it otherwise. Privacy is extremely rare, and apparently unwanted. "But won't you be lonely?" is the most common remark the foreigner hears when he announces his intention of having a room to himself.

But while they seek physical proximity, the Japanese are short on comradeship. The family, although traditionally revered as an institution, tends to be a rather cool arrangement, and a hierarchic one. The notion that everyone will gather around the dinner table at a fixed time of the evening is not central to it as it is to the American family. The members tend to straggle in and out whenever they please, and sometimes the father is not seen at dinner for days on end.

A man's lifetime friends tend to be from his high school days, if he has had high school days. For this brief period of springtime revelry, comradeship as equals is possible. If such comradeship may be described as a horizontal relationship, vertical relationships become common thereafter. These are the much stiffer and more restrained relations of junior to senior and inferior to superior, which exist within the closed hierarchy of a company, a university, or even a political party or philanthropic organization. A British delegate to the 1960 convention of the Inter-Parliamentary Union, held in Tokyo, expressed astonishment at the fact that two Japanese delegates would not ride in the same car if they belonged to different parties. Had he pursued the matter further, he might have found members of different factions within the same party behaving in a similar fashion. The tight faction, as suspicious of outsiders as one tomcat is of another, is at once a curse and a blessing for Japanese society. It is a curse because it militates against broader humanity, a blessing because pride of faction can be a disciplining force and an incentive to achievement.

FOR this diagnosis of Japanese social relationships, one need not trust only to observation. There is also the authority of eminent Japanese literary critics, who think that the lack of "horizontal" relationships has limited Japanese writers to a narrow view, and turned many of them to the somewhat pale autobiographical writing that is so prominent in modern Japanese letters. Whether or not it is an adequate explanation, the want is certainly to be remarked upon. Easy social intercourse is rare. One can almost hear a sigh of relief when a child toddles into a roomful of adults and they can turn their attention from one another to the youngster. A person sometimes hears this remark from a Japanese who has traveled abroad: "When I am walking down the street and see a light in a western house, I feel warm. When I see a light in a Japanese house, I feel cold."

The foreigner who complains, "But I just can't get in with them," should not worry too much about the failure. They have trouble getting in with themselves.

The Spell of a Vanishing Loveliness

"Remember that here all is enchantment,—that you have fallen under the spell of the dead,—that the lights and the colours and the voices must fade away at last into emptiness and silence." So wrote Lafcadio Hearn, the Greek-born mystic who, after many years in America, found his spiritual home in Japan more than half a century ago. Longing for times and things past lingers on in modern Japan, which is still in transition between East and West, between old and new, between medieval countryside and pulsating 20th Century urban life. For the Japanese past commingles with the present day and flows on into the future. Age-old customs and habits of life are full of vitality, and there still persists what Hearn called "the viewless pressure of numberless vanished generations." So in spite of radical changes caused by war and economic revolution, Japan continues to bewitch the world with the modesty of its women, the artistry of its gardens, the mystery of its shrines and the magic contours of its hills and valleys.

17

Carrying gay parasols, mothers in kimonos accompany their children, who wear western-style clothes, along a country road to school.

18

Spring rains brighten the fields, where yellow mustard and green barley sprout in a soil more closely tilled than any other on earth

19

WORLDLY PLEASURES (*opposite*) lure nighttime throngs past the neon signs of Tokyo's Asakusa quarter, where triple-feature movies, teahouses and jazz clubs seek trade.

SACRED SHRINE honoring Tokugawa Ieyasu draws sightseers along a lantern-lined avenue in Ueno Park, Tokyo, to pay their homage to the great 17th Century statesman.

HILL FARM wears a crown of gracefully blossoming cherry. Here time seems at a standstill for the farmer's wife, who feeds her chickens with corn dried under the eaves of an old thatched barn. Today, however, country folk are drifting into the towns in search of a far easier and more exciting way of life.

22

2

The Heritage of a Long Isolation

JAPAN before the 19th Century was a country uniquely free from foreign wars. Only twice did the Japanese try to take part of the continent, and only once was there a threat that Japan itself would be invaded. Through the centuries the Japanese people were free to develop an independent nation, and to borrow ideas and institutions from neighboring peoples. China did borrow a gadget from Japan now and then (the contribution of which the Japanese seem proudest is the folding fan). But Japan for its part borrowed a civilization—and from a country which, unlike Rome, made no attempt to impose it by force.

Much of pre-modern Japanese history can be understood as an interplay between the indigenous and the foreign—not as a mechanical interplay, with one rhythmically rising as the other rhythmically falls, but rather as a process whereby a stubbornly native element continues to assert itself despite a flood of borrowing. In the Seventh and Eighth Centuries the Japanese were willing borrowers from China; a second period of borrowing from China reached a climax in the 15th Century; and in the past century the Japanese have been equally receptive toward influences from the West. In between, there have been periods of consolidation and withdrawal, generally involving only the interruption of official intercourse with foreign countries, but once—from the mid-17th Century to the mid-19th—going to the extreme of virtually complete isolation.

When the West arrived in the 19th Century and would not be put out, the Japanese were uniquely prepared to make the necessary adjustments. They had had much experience with digesting alien civilizations. Throughout their history they had taken techniques from abroad and shaped them to the native spirit, and it was not hard for them to adopt new techniques and customs from the West as they had once assimilated new ways from China.

BEFORE the Japanese wrote their own history the country was mentioned in Chinese and Korean chronicles. By the beginning of the Christian era some concentration of power had been built up in the Kyoto-Osaka area. In the Fourth Century an invasion was mounted against Korea, and the Japanese retained a foothold there until the Seventh Century. By the Sixth Century, when Buddhism was imported from Korea, the principal clan in the Kyoto-Osaka area had achieved ascendancy over sizable portions of central Japan, and had sufficient prestige to call its chiefs the rulers of the land. Their family still occupies the Japanese throne.

The country was far from united, however. Local aristocrats continued to be powerful, and at places remote from the "capital" they were completely independent. The capital and the court were themselves rather insubstantial affairs. It was the practice to move the court upon an emperor's death, so that capitals were at various times in the Osaka-Nara area and as far north as Lake Biwa, east of Kyoto.

With the importation of Buddhism, the first great flood of culture started from China, coming by way of Korea. Most ably encouraged by Prince Shōtoku, the great statesman of Seventh Century Japan, the nobility began wearing Chinese robes and building Chinese buildings, and in theory they adopted a centralized Chinese administrative system and a Chinese system of land tenure. The court presently settled in Nara. The central clan announced somewhat cavalierly that the lands of the realm were now its to dispose of, and the landowning nobility were given court ranks by way of compensation. Actually, as will be apparent in a moment, the high-spirited clans were probably able to keep the facts of land tenure from squaring with the theory.

SO great was the prestige of the Chinese language in this period that it was uncertain whether or not the Japanese language would ever become an important literary medium. So complex had the Japanese written language become because of the adapting of characters from the Chinese (a language wholly alien to it) that the arguments were compelling for using Chinese instead.

Yet Japanese culture did grow into something more than just another form of provincial Chinese culture. Beginning in the late Ninth Century, when official relations with China were broken off, the native spirit began to reassert itself. One important statesman may be taken as a symbol of the change: Sugawara Michizane. He was responsible for discontinuing embassies to China, and he is credited with having invented the expression, "Chinese learning, Japanese spirit." Since his meteoric career made him for a time the most powerful person in the land but ended in his being exiled, he is a melancholy sort of hero, and the Japanese love to invent stories about him. But even if he did not coin the phrase, the attribution of it to him is symbolically proper. At about the time official embassies were stopped, a native spirit was indeed asserting itself, a force which was to shape the imported learning into something original.

Actually the Japanese spirit had been present all along. From the start, the Chinese administrative system had never really worked. The economic and institutional history of the country from the Seventh Century to the 12th can be seen as the emergence of Japanese fact over Chinese theory. Whatever the country's rulers said about the matter, the regional nobility in fact held lands beyond the power of the capital to control. By the 12th Century the court was merely one owner of land rights among many, and could do next to nothing about lands not its own. The spirit of the Japanese clans, truculent and divisive, had kept Chinese institutions from working.

MEANWHILE, about the time of the break with China, the cultural flowering of the great Heian Period was getting under way. The Japanese capital was moved from Nara to Kyoto in the late Eighth Century, and there, in the following centuries, a small coterie of court nobles set about deliberately cultivating good taste. In the process they created the finest literature and some of the finest art that have ever come out of Japan.

Whereas "Chinese learning" can be rather neatly defined, "Japanese spirit" is wholly elusive. The first phrase applies to a philosophical tradition, either Buddhist or Confucian, and to advanced scholarship in fields like medicine and philology. The second is much vaguer—a touch, a feeling, an intuitive assertion. In the Heian Period, for example, one looks in vain for an adventurous, restless and exploring mind. Heian inclinations were predominantly esthetic. The typical intellectual was an adapter and not a pioneer, and the finest energies of the period went into putting together harmonious colors, syllables, perfumes or lines of ink. Perhaps nowhere else at any other time has so much careful attention been devoted to choosing an undergarment or so much time put into dispatching a love note, always exquisite down to the last detail, with perhaps a tastefully faded chrysanthemum to emphasize the melancholy nature of the contents. And never was there a society

MAJOR PERIODS OF JAPANESE HISTORY

ARCHAIC PERIOD (Before 552 A.D.)

Peoples from the Asian mainland, ranging from Manchuria to Southeast Asia, settle in Japan. Country becomes partially unified around the start of the Fourth Century.

ASUKA PERIOD (552-710)

Buddhism is introduced from China. The state is ruled from Asuka in Yamato province. A code of laws is introduced. Strong Buddhist influence on the arts.

'NARA PERIOD (710-794)

The first permanent capital is built at Nara. Buddhism wins wide acceptance. A budding Japanese culture comes under the powerful influence of Chinese culture.

HEIAN PERIOD (794-1185)

The capital is moved to a new city near Nara called Heian-kyo (now Kyoto). Native art and literature flourish. Power shifts from the emperor to the Fujiwara family.

KAMAKURA PERIOD (1185-1333)

The first of the shoguns, Minamoto Yoritomo, governs from Kamakura (though the imperial court stays in Kyoto). Zen Buddhism develops. Mongols fail to take Japan.

MUROMACHI PERIOD (1333-1568)

The Muromachi shogunate brings the effective capital back to Kyoto. The Nō drama and the tea ceremony are developed. St. Francis Xavier introduces Christianity.

AZUCHI-MOMOYAMA PERIOD (1568-1600)

Civil wars divide Japan, but the country is finally unified by Hideyoshi. Unsuccessful Korean invasion. Ieyasu, founder of Tokugawa shogunate, succeeds Hideyoshi.

EDO or TOKUGAWA PERIOD (1600-1868)

Tokugawa Ieyasu moves the government administration to Edo (now Tokyo). Christianity is suppressed. Japan's isolation ends only with Perry's arrival in 1853.

MEIJI PERIOD (1868-1912)

Under Emperor Meiji, Japan adopts western-style reforms and begins a program of territorial expansion. Japan defeats China, and Russia and becomes a world power.

TAISHO AND SHOWA PERIODS (1912—)

Expansionism in 1930s leads to defeat in 1945. "Taishō" and "Shōwa" are names given posthumously to emperors (Hirohito's reign will be called the Shōwa Period).

in which the color blind, the tremulous of the hand or the uncomely of countenance were more hopelessly out of place.

The Japanese spirit made itself known in another way. As early as the Nara Period, control of the country, insofar as it was centrally controlled, had slipped from the hands of the emperors to the first of the great families who for most of the next thousand years were to rule in the emperor's name. Real power was to be in the hands of civil regents, such as the Fujiwara family of the Heian Period, or of military dictators called shoguns—the Minamoto family, the Ashikaga, the Tokugawa.

When one or another of these families was not in control, various combinations of events prevented vigorous rule by the emperor. Sometimes there were civil wars, so that no one was in complete control. Sometimes a retired emperor took advantage of his freedom from ceremonial duties to control the titular emperor. In the most characteristically Japanese fashion of all, there were on occasion complexes of power three and four layers thick: on the throne would be an emperor, behind whom would be a retired emperor theoretically wielding power in his name, behind whom would be a titular shogun, behind whom would be a regent—the actual wielder of power.

By the end of the Heian Period—toward the close of the 12th Century—the court nobility no longer had any influence on lands except, precariously, its own. The assumption that the central government could allot and tax land was at an end, and with it the attempt to impose a Chinese land system. Meanwhile regional clans had become aware of their power, and war broke out between the two strongest, the Taira and the Minamoto, to decide who should make a new beginning toward a central government.

JAPANESE PROPER NAMES

The Japanese have always listed proper names by putting the family name first, the given name second. The famous Minamoto brothers of the 12th Century are thus recorded in history as Minamoto Yoritomo and Minamoto Yoshitsune. Throughout this chapter alone, Japanese names are given in this traditional manner. But in the rest of the book, to simplify matters for the average reader, the western style is followed, with the family name last.

No other disturbance in Japanese history has so excited the national imagination. The story of the brief rise to glory and precipitous fall of the Taira clan has been the source of countless tales and plays. So has the temporary eclipse and subsequent rise to power of the Minamoto clan. From the defeat of the Taira comes the archetypal story of the mighty driven from power and dispersed, and there are villages scattered over Japan and down into the Ryukyu Islands whose inhabitants still claim to be descended from Taira refugees.

The Minamoto clan simultaneously produced one of the most ruthlessly talented men in all Japanese history and one of the most tragically talented: the half brothers Yoritomo and Yoshitsune. Yoritomo's was the master hand guiding the Minamoto rise to power, and Yoshitsune was his most capable general. After the Taira were defeated once and for all, Yoshitsune himself became a threat to Yoritomo, and so, with his companion Benkei, the warrior was hounded over the country, eventually to commit suicide. Proud and tight-lipped, Yoritomo is immortalized in a portrait that is one of the masterpieces of Japanese art. Benkei and Yoshitsune also survive: they are among the best-loved characters of the Japanese stage.

Granted the title of shogun by the emperor, Yoritomo set up his headquarters at Kamakura, south of present-day Tokyo. The Kamakura shogunate, in power until the early 14th Century, began cautiously to assert a unifying influence once more. The process continued through the early years of the Muromachi shogunate, which succeeded the Kamakura shogunate and brought the effective capital back to Kyoto.

For Kyoto, this move was unfortunate. In the mid-15th Century, fighting broke out between rival factions of the shogunate, and the result was to destroy the shogunate itself as anything more than one regional power among many —and, in the process, to destroy Kyoto. The civil wars went on for more than a hundred years. In Kyoto today, except for a few outlying areas, there is no building left from the great Heian Period.

IF the centuries of civil war were cruel and violent, they were also a time of cultural activity. Much of it was under the influence of China, for this was a second period of energetic borrowing from the continent. This time, however, the Chinese flood did not pour in on a primitive and unlettered country, but on a country that was beginning to acquire a sense of its own past. There was no danger that the native culture would go under. When the country was at length unified at the end of the 16th Century, peace brought an outburst of artistic gaiety in which the Japanese spirit was triumphant. The bold yet harmonious colors of the Nijō Castle in Kyoto, for example, could only be Japanese.

Japan emerged from the civil wars with something else: a highly developed commercial economy and a buoyant, expansionist mercantile spirit. This was the day that saw Japan's second invasion of Korea. The horrors of this 16th Century invasion have become a part of Korean folklore. Almost no Korean public building predates the 16th Century. The Japanese apparently set the torch to everything they came upon.

Although this political invasion shortly came to an end, a commercial invasion of Asia was also taking place. By the end of the 16th Century, Japanese traders were roaming Southeast Asia, the Indies and the Philippines. Moving down on the winds from Siberia, their ships would go south in the autumn, to return on the early summer monsoon. There were Japanese settlements in Annam, Cambodia and Siam as well as in the Philippines, and the Japanese were so active in the East Indies that the Dutch found them valuable as agents and labor contractors. Several thousand Japanese seem to have been resident in Manila, where the Spanish kept them

fairly well out of politics. In other places they had more freedom for their energies. One remarkable Japanese even became viceroy of Siam early in the 17th Century.

Had the process been allowed to continue, the commercial empires of the East and the West might have struck a precarious balance in southern Asia, with neither clearly in control. But on that, one can only speculate, for Japanese activities abroad came to an abrupt halt. Beginning in the middle of the 17th Century, Japan virtually closed itself off from the world. Its far-flung traders either came home or were absorbed into the cultures of their various adopted countries, and Japanese history became a cramped, insular affair for two centuries. At the end of this time, Japan was far behind the rest of the world in technical matters, and the final confrontation with the West in the middle of the 19th Century took place not in southern Asia but on Japanese shores, with Japan much the weaker of the two parties.

FOR the story of this crucial withdrawal from the world it is necessary to return to domestic matters. When the civil wars at last came to an end in the latter half of the 16th Century, three great men could claim credit for the peace. The first, Oda Nobunaga, was originally a minor military leader from the Nagoya region, but by his 30th year he controlled much of central Japan, and by his 40th he had disposed of the last Muromachi shogun. By 1582, the year of his assassination at the age of 48, he was as near as anyone had been for more than a century to controlling the whole country.

He was succeeded as shogun by Toyotomi Hideyoshi, the prime example of a self-made man in Japanese history. Hideyoshi was the son of a minor vassal of Nobunaga, but had such talent that he early won the confidence of his chief and, upon Nobunaga's death, emerged as his successor. He continued the conquest of Japan and finally brought it under complete control a decade later. Hideyoshi's last important act was the unsuccessful invasion of Korea mentioned previously. When he died in 1598, only one major problem faced the country: Would his heirs preside over Japan or would those of his ablest lieutenant, Tokugawa Ieyasu? In the struggle for power which ensued, the victory went to Ieyasu, the third great figure of this period, and in 1615 the last resistance ended with the fall of what had been Hideyoshi's main stronghold, Osaka Castle.

All three men could be cruel and treacherous. Nobunaga ordered the destruction of the huge monastery on Mount Hiei, northeast of Kyoto, and the slaughter of every monk his men came upon; Hideyoshi forced the suicide of his own stepson; Ieyasu turned upon the weak heir of his former master and took Osaka Castle by resort to the most repellent deceit. Yet they were all great warriors, and, by coincidence, able administrators as well. When Ieyasu finally established his shogunate in Edo—present-day Tokyo—he governed a relatively unified country. If the emergence of a centralized state is one mark of modernization, then it may be said that Japan was launched on that course well over two centuries before the West finally appeared on the scene.

THE West had already come once, and its arrival had helped to produce the Tokugawa administration's decision to close the country. The pioneering Jesuit, St. Francis Xavier, had reached Japan in 1549. There followed "Japan's Christian century," which ended, after years of persecution, with a Christian rebellion in 1637 and the virtual exclusion of Europeans from the country. After 1640 only a few Dutch traders remained, on a tiny island in Nagasaki harbor.

Disagreements within the Catholic Church, which was in many ways its own worst enemy in Japan, had given the Japanese authorities cause to suspect that religious penetration by outsiders was a prelude to political penetration. The Christian missionaries had come at an unfortunate time, when the civil wars inevitably brought them into Japanese politics. The ultimate victor, Tokugawa Ieyasu, had reason to believe that they had trucked with his enemies. Yet it is possible that the country might have been closed even if there had been no missionaries at all. The Tokugawa shoguns had a notion that society could be kept from changing, even while the roving merchant class was busy changing it. Quite possibly, therefore, the shoguns would have made the merchants come home and closed the country in any case.

IN Edo the Tokugawa shoguns set up a regime with some of the attributes of modern dictatorship. There were controls on traveling, the military barons were required to maintain houses in Edo where their families became hostages, and the lower classes were organized into small groups which were held responsible as groups for the misbehavior of their members. (The clannishness and factionalism of the Japanese today may perhaps in part be traced back to this system.) Even religion was put to the service of the government. Everyone had to register with a temple, and the registration became a means of control.

Society was divided into four classes: the warrior (the samurai whom Americans learned about during World War II was a lesser member of this class), the farmer, the artisan and the merchant. Much of Tokugawa economic history can be read as a conflict between the theory of a *static* society and the fact of a *changing* society. Theoretically, the merchants were the lowest of the four classes. In reality they were economically the most powerful. The shogunate assumed that merchants were beneath the proud warriors' notice, an assumption which did not encourage a search for a solution to the problems posed by the merchants' presence.

Modern Japan inherited a code of behavior imposed by the Tokugawa shogunate. Loyalty was considered the first of all virtues. To this end the shogunate imported from China a variety of Confucianism which in the Japanese version neglected metaphysics and emphasized a secular code built around hierarchic relationships of inferior to superior (wife to husband, son to father, vassal to lord and the like), and around the obligations of the former to the latter. When the strange notion of inalienable

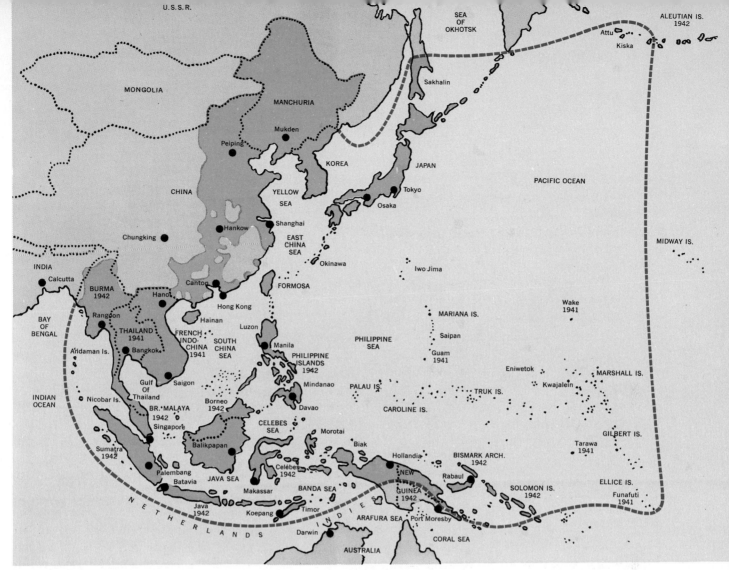

MAP LABELS:
U.S.S.R.
SEA OF OKHOTSK
ALEUTIAN IS. 1942
Attu
Kiska
MONGOLIA
MANCHURIA
Sakhalin
Mukden
Peiping
KOREA
JAPAN
PACIFIC OCEAN
CHINA
YELLOW SEA
Tokyo
Osaka
Hankow
Shanghai
EAST CHINA SEA
Chungking
Okinawa
MIDWAY IS.
INDIA
Calcutta
Canton
FORMOSA
Iwo Jima
BURMA 1942
Hanoi
Hong Kong
BAY OF BENGAL
Rangoon
Hainan
Luzon
Wake 1941
THAILAND 1941
FRENCH INDO-CHINA 1941
SOUTH CHINA SEA
Manila
MARIANA IS.
Andaman Is.
Bangkok
PHILIPPINE ISLANDS 1942
Saipan
PHILIPPINE SEA
Guam 1941
Eniwetok
MARSHALL IS.
Gulf Of Thailand
Saigon
Mindanao
PALAU IS.
TRUK IS.
Kwajalein
INDIAN OCEAN
Nicobar Is.
BR. MALAYA 1942
Borneo 1942
Davao
CAROLINE IS.
Singapore
CELEBES SEA
Morotai
Biak
GILBERT IS.
Sumatra 1942
Balikpapan
Celébes 1942
Hollandia
BISMARCK ARCH. 1942
Tarawa 1941
Palembang
Batavia
JAVA SEA
Makassar
BANDA SEA
NEW GUINEA 1942
Rabaul
SOLOMON IS. 1942
ELLICE IS.
Funafuti 1941
NETHERLANDS
Java 1942
Koepang
Timor
ARAFURA SEA
Port Moresby
INDIES
Darwin
AUSTRALIA
CORAL SEA

THE JAPANESE EMPIRE at its zenith during World War II is shown above, with the dates when the territories were acquired. The dotted line marks the farthest Japanese military advance. Beginning in 1942, counterattacks by U.S. and other forces turned the Japanese back, and at the end of the war they controlled only their home islands.

rights for all was imported into Japan in the 19th Century, a new word had to be coined for putting it into Japanese.

The Tokugawa Japanese was a secularized person who looked not to gods but to his superior. The one absolute was that the superior's interests must be served. This way of thinking and behaving is one of the keys to the sudden shifts of which the Japanese are capable. The interests of the emperor as head of the family-state came first—for was it not he, rather than the shogun, who was the final object of the cult of loyalty? His interests, and the nation's, took precedence even if they meant reversing national policies overnight.

The reversal occurred when Commodore Matthew Perry of the U.S. Navy, charged with making arrangements for trade with Japan, appeared in Edo Bay with four ships on a summer day in 1853. He was accosting a nation that may have preferred, with half its heart, to stay out of the world, but a nation that need not have been wholly taken by surprise. The Russians had been trying for more than half a century to open relations. The King of the Netherlands, through his traders in Nagasaki, had tried to warn the shogunate of what was coming. When the Millard Fillmore administration decided to dispatch the Perry mission to Japan, it informed the Dutch Foreign Ministry of its intentions and the message was passed along to Nagasaki.

In a broader sense, Perry came upon a nation that was ready for change. Insularity was by the end of the 18th Century beginning to give Japanese culture a tired, warmed-over look. Art and literature were for the most part repeating old themes. And the Tokugawa shoguns had indoctrinated the nation in a code of ethics that would remain intact and provide an essential stability and discipline even if the shoguns were to disappear.

Disappear they did. The trade treaty with Perry set off a train of circumstances beyond the shogunate's control. In 1867 and 1868 the last shogun resigned, his followers were subdued and the young Emperor Meiji, whose ancestors for centuries had wielded almost no power over affairs of state, moved from Kyoto to Edo. Edo thus became Tokyo (Eastern Capital) and the "Meiji Restoration" was accomplished.

The reign of Meiji, from 1867 to 1912, was pre-eminently the day of what the American economist Thorstein Veblen was to call "the opportunity of Japan," a period when the disciplines instilled under the shoguns could be put to the uses of modern technology. The story of modern Japan is the story of what happened to the old discipline and what was done with the new techniques.

MEIJI himself was a shadowy figure, and the vast majority of his subjects never looked upon him and never heard his voice. To them he was a god. They stared at the ground when he passed, and he did not condescend to make speeches. It is as a symbol, rather, that he is important. When Meiji came to the throne in 1867 as a boy of 15, Japan was powerless to turn away foreign incursions, and had been forced into a series of "unequal treaties" which limited the power of Japanese courts of law and denied the country tariff autonomy. By the time he died in 1912, a group of remarkable leaders, chiefly from the southwestern clans that had been the strongest forces behind the Meiji Restoration, had accomplished their purpose. The country was secure; the unequal treaties

were gone and Japan was instead allied as an equal with England. Two great neighboring powers, China and Russia, had been defeated by Japan. Korea and Formosa had been taken over. And—a sign that Meiji leaders were more flexible than Tokugawa leaders—the earliest representative parliament outside the western world had been operating for more than two decades.

THE Meiji Period was a time of hope, courage, youthful vitality and growth. It was a long success story, and a period which the Japanese continue to regard with great affection. One of the most famous modern Japanese poetic aphorisms goes like this:

Snow is falling.
Meiji recedes in the distance.

One may imagine the poet looking out as snow falls on the roofs of a later, dirtier and less buoyant Tokyo, and thinking of that better day now disappearing into the past.

Even by the end of the Meiji Period, however, the old discipline was beginning to crack. Subordination within the family had been central to the Tokugawa code, but early 20th Century Japanese novels were highly critical of the family. With the advent of World War I the urbanization of Japan began to leap ahead, and by 1923, the year of the great earthquake, Tokyo was a city of four million people, or twice what it had been in 1900.

Meanwhile Marxism had entered the country, and with it class warfare. The loosening of the old restraints brought Japan a flapper era, when "cafés" appeared on the Ginza to satisfy every carnal appetite and the "modern girl" tried to look and act like a Hollywood star. It was also a period of democratic experiment, when universal manhood suffrage came to Japan.

A decade after the war, the national economy began to be caught up in the international depression. It was obvious that the unity of Meiji no longer existed, for in the unhappy decade of the 1930s, terrorism, manifesting itself in a series of assassinations and attempted assassinations, gave evidence of deep national divisions.

The foreign adventures of the decade, the invasion of Manchuria in 1931 and the invasion of China proper in 1937, did not have behind them a country united as it had been united against the Russians some three decades earlier.

The most recent phase of Japan's history is familiar to most Americans. After Japan's attack on Pearl Harbor late in 1941, the country's military and naval forces swept through the South Pacific and Southeast Asia. In the spring of 1942, when the last defenders of the Philippines surrendered, the Japanese were on the borders of India and were almost within jumping-off distance of Australia. By the spring of 1945 the Americans had landed on Okinawa, one of the Japanese home prefectures, and all of the main Japanese cities except Kyoto were in ruins. Then came the atomic bomb, and at noon on August 15 a stunned nation, which had never before heard his voice (he was as distant as Meiji had been), was told by Emperor Hirohito that it had been defeated. On August 30, General Douglas MacArthur landed southwest of Tokyo, and the task of reorganizing and rebuilding began.

WHAT went wrong? Why did the youthful ebullience of the Meiji Period lead to the disaster of 1945? Was it because of something unchanged in Japan since the Meiji Restoration of 1867 and 1868? Or might it have been because of something that happened later, because of certain perils that lie waiting for all peoples somewhere along the way to urbanization and industrialization, and which some are luckier at avoiding than others?

Those who blame the World War II defeat on something left over from pre-modern Japan characteristically offer a Marxist explanation. They regard the history of a nation as an inevitable progression through various stages known as "feudalism" and "bourgeois democracy" or "capitalism" to "socialism." From this theory they advance the notion that Japanese expansionism, which led to the debacle of 1945, was caused by "feudal remnants," centered in the imperial household.

It is impossible to deny the importance of the imperial institution. But to say that the Japanese fought for the emperor is to say that they were impelled by patriotism, which is not to say much of anything at all. The imperial system had changed a great deal by 1945. The young officers who had been responsible for the violence of the 1930s did not consider the wishes of the emperor, and in 1945 the most violent of them sought by force to prevent the emperor's surrender broadcast, even though in recording that broadcast he had made his wishes quite clear. In brief, though the trappings of divinity remained until the beginning of 1946, the emperor was already well on the way to becoming what the new Constitution tells us he is, merely "the symbol of the State."

Those who advance the theory of "feudal remains" also do the Japanese a disservice by neglecting the steps toward democracy which prewar Japan had taken. Parliamentary processes had been formally respected through the 1930s —even when the Diet voted itself out of business—and the notion of democracy as something good, if not wholly practical in Japan, had been widespread by the end of the 1920s.

If, then, the Marxist notion of "feudal remains" is not enough to explain the phenomenon of Japanese expansionism, what is a better explanation? To some extent the country's performance need not be described as expansionism at all, but rather as national self-defense, a way of forestalling rivals.

YET when all allowances are made, history will record that much of what the Japanese did was cruel and greedy. To be sure, other nations were cruel and greedy at the same time. And if their behavior is not also to be blamed on "feudal remnants," it seems possible that similar forces led them all astray. In the end, it may be that the heritage of the Tokugawa Period was no more important than the vast phenomena known as urbanization and modernization. These have sent more countries than Japan on the way to expansion, and will probably send still more in the future.

Seagirt Bastion Against Invaders

Snug for centuries behind its ocean moat, Japan has never in recorded history been successfully invaded by force of arms. What might have been invasion in 1945 was averted by surrender. Previously, however, one major threat of conquest occurred. In 1274, Kublai

In a 13th Century scroll sequence, the Japanese general Kagesuke prepares for battle

Japanese guards man the fortifications, while

Mongol bowmen bring down a Japanese horseman riding out to halt the invasion

Takesaki Suyenaga and his soldiers board a

Khan, given immortality by the poet Coleridge as the Mongol emperor of China who built a "stately pleasure dome," dispatched an expedition which was routed. He tried again in 1281, but after some land and sea affrays (*below*) his fleet was destroyed by a typhoon. Thereafter, until the arrival of America's Commodore Matthew Perry in 1853, no foreign warships reached Japan. But the tide changed in the late 19th Century, when Japan began its own expansion.

the cavalry sallies forth to attack the invaders

Mounted archers charge the Mongols after a flanking movement through the forest

Mongol warship and engage in a fierce battle

Japanese soldiers board the Mongol flagship and fight the enemy at close quarters

ON THE EVE of Japan's awakening, Commodore Perry lands at the treaty port of Shimoda in 1854 with a display of force to overawe the shogun's emissaries. Two years later, Townsend Harris, first U.S. Consul General to Japan, raised his flag in the same port. The lithograph is by Wilhelm Heine, official artist of the Perry expedition.

AT THE DAWN of his nation's advent to world power, Emperor Meiji (*right*), maker of modern Japan, heads his victorious cavalry after the defeat of China in 1895.

A GIANT LEAP *out of the backward past into modern times made Japan the rival of the advanced nations of the West*

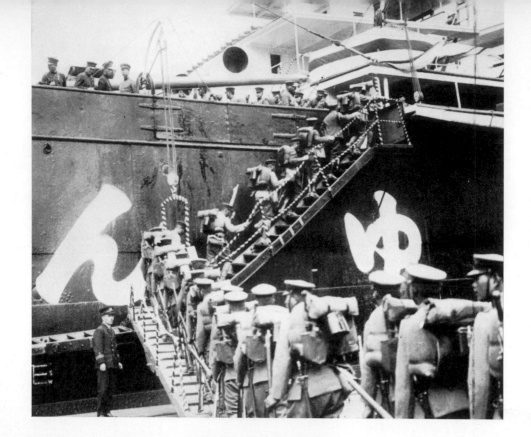

BOUND FOR MANCHURIA in 1931, crack Japanese soldiers embark on a transport. Japan's move was one of many aggressive acts by totalitarian powers before World War II.

IN CHINA, a local collaborator (*left*) blots out the British flag on the door of a building in Hankow in 1938. Japanese expansion continued uninterruptedly until 1942.

AT HOME, Tokyo's own elite First Division (*right*) parades in triumph through the capital in 1936, before sailing for Manchuria and the major Japanese invasion of China.

AFTERMATH OF DEFEAT *brought its toll of lives and cities*

WAR-WEARY SOLDIERS on the way home in 1945 alight from a troop train in the Hiroshima station and view the ruins of the first city devastated by the atom's power.

CAREFREE CHILDREN (*opposite*) today enjoy a playground in the center of Hiroshima, where only the Industry Promotion Hall (*center background*) withstood the blast.

3

Storm and Calm in Politics

TODAY, more than a decade and a half since the surrender, Japan presents the extraordinary picture of a country that seems unable to answer the fundamental questions about what it is and where it is going, and yet seems to go on as if the questions did not require answers. On the one hand we have the placid face of Japan, a nation building and working, generally staying out of the world's way and repeatedly electing comfortable conservative majorities to

its Diet. On the other we have the distraught face, breaking into hysteria when some basic decision approaches about the nation's place in the world.

Seven years of American occupation did not make of the Japanese a nation wholly committed to the western cause. Yet the Occupation may claim much credit for the placid face of Japan. When General Douglas MacArthur landed at Atsugi Airfield, a dazed and frightened nation awaited him. The task was to rebuild and to reorganize.

At first the emphasis was less on rebuilding than on reorganizing. The initial statement of post-surrender policy, prepared by America's State, War and Navy Departments and radioed in substance to General MacArthur the day before he flew to Japan, was, understandably, a somewhat vindictive document. The ultimate objectives were to make sure that Japan would "not again become a menace to the United States or to the peace and security of the world," and to establish "a peaceful and responsible government." The means toward that end were for the most part political: disarmament, restriction of sovereignty to the main home islands, and the encouragement of "a desire for individual liberties." Somewhat grudgingly, a fourth means was added: the development of an economy to satisfy "the peacetime requirements of the population." Lest this fourth means give the Japanese extravagant ideas, however, a stern warning was handed down later in the document: "The plight of Japan is the direct outcome of its own behavior, and the Allies will not undertake the burden of repairing the damage."

By the outbreak of the Korean War in 1950, the emphasis had shifted to economic recovery. As early as 1948 the intention to make the shift had been clear: the Secretary of the Army, Kenneth Royall, made a speech declaring that changes in the world situation had brought a need for changes in policy toward Japan. The country must be allowed to stand on its own feet as a barrier against the Communist threat in Asia.

THIS shift in policy has often been called a reversal of policy. The articulate intelligentsia of Japan, who are overwhelmingly in favor of the Occupation reforms but reluctant to see their country become a "bastion of democracy" in the Far East if that means involvement in further international strife, continue to blame the "reversal" on the Americans, and so to blame them for the growth of anti-American

sentiment in the late Occupation and post-Occupation years. To most Americans, however, the change in policy was a shift and not a reversal, for the ultimate goals remained the same: peace and security. As America's wartime anger faded, the threat from a revived Japan seemed to shrink into insignificance, while the threat from the two great antidemocratic powers on the continent was growing enormously.

In its reforming years, down to 1948, the Occupation undertook a great deal. Acting through the Japanese Diet, it transferred the ownership of cultivated land from landlord to tenant farmer. It passed legislation attempting to do much the same thing with fishing rights. It gave women the vote. It revised the legal codes to emphasize equal rights and imposed a new constitution with a similar emphasis. It revised the educational system to be more like that of the United States both in its structure and in the accepted methods of teaching. It removed many restrictions on the right to strike and encouraged the labor movement. It purged wartime leaders in the hope that younger leaders would emerge to take their places. It dissolved ultra-nationalist organizations, and set about breaking up excessive concentrations of power in business and finance.

BUT the Occupation had shortcomings, and the greatest of these was a want of modesty. In this it showed how much it was the creature of its leader. Simultaneously austere and flamboyant, with a fine knack for rhetoric and a genius for seeming almost divinely remote, General MacArthur was an imaginative and far-sighted statesman. Given his energies and his powerful personality, he could have sabotaged Washington's program for occupied Japan most effectively, had he been of a mind to do so. Instead he made the program his own—so effectively that Japanese and Americans alike tended to forget both that the policy did in fact come from Washington and that the history of democratic Japan had not begun with MacArthur. For he was not a modest leader. The great claims his Occupation made for itself rather tempted the observer, out of sheer perversity, to point out that Japan took its first steps toward democracy when General MacArthur was still in grammar school, and that certain Occupation reforms were complete failures.

Among the failures may be counted the attempt to bring about economic decentralization, which will be discussed in a later chapter; the fisheries reform, which did not take into consideration the capital needs of marine enterprises; and the purge of wartime leaders. Three post-Occupation prime ministers were men who had been purged, and one of them, Nobusuke Kishi, had been so deeply involved in Japan's military adventuring that he had spent some years in prison awaiting trial as a war criminal (he was eventually released without having been tried).

OTHER reforms must be described as mixed successes. Undeniably a vigorous labor movement was established, but it would be difficult to say that a crop of cool and farsighted union leaders was produced to guide it. Most of them are militant Marxists. Again, it is undeniable that teaching techniques in Japanese schools are now considerably nearer the American pattern than they used to be; but one wonders how much difference techniques make when the teachers are controlled by a Marxist union.

After all of these shortcomings are taken into account, however, much remains. Leftist critics carp at the land reform because it did not also divide up forest land, and recent surveys by the Ministry of Agriculture suggest some tendency on the part of the very small farmer to give up and sell out to a larger neighbor. But the reform nonetheless did remove the landlord problem, and it gave Japan a huge class of farmer-owners, whose political strength will make any tampering with the land laws very difficult. Women have the vote, and though they may complain of continuing inequalities, no one is likely to deprive them of the right to press for change through the polls. And, whether or not the Occupation can claim credit, the ultra-nationalism of the 1930s has been

fully discredited, and it only becomes more discredited when its latter-day adherents encourage such acts of violence as the assassination in 1960 of a Socialist politician.

The most basic of the Occupation reforms concerned the nation's laws: the rewriting of the legal codes and the promulgation of a new constitution. In both cases the emphasis was on rights instead of duties, and upon equality as opposed to the old hierarchical arrangements. Once again, however, it must be pointed out that the Americans did not come up with much that the Japanese had not thought of before.

To take an example: the Civil Code of 1948 virtually did away with the old-style, authoritarian family as a legal unit and hence with the authority of its head. It improved the positions of the family's weaker members by abolishing primogeniture and by allowing a wife the grounds for divorce which until then only her husband had possessed. But the new code was merely an extension of a way of thought that had been current in Japan since at least the end of World War I, when a special commission to study family problems had been established.

These facts are introduced not to belittle the accomplishments of the Occupation, but rather to suggest that the reforms may have lasting effects because they have played on old native sympathies. Indeed it may be that, when the final history of the episode is written, the attempt of the Occupation to weaken the family system will prove its most significant act.

THE new Japanese Constitution was drafted by Occupation officials early in 1946, and translated into Japanese. Aside from the fact that it states the principles of equality and individual rights elaborated in the legal codes, it is interesting chiefly for its embodiment of the very early Occupation spirit, when a revival of Japanese militarism was considered the chief threat to peace in the Far East. The strangest and most controversial provision of the Constitution, Article 9, should be quoted in full:

Aspiring sincerely to an international peace based on justice and order, the Japanese people forever renounce war as a sovereign right of the nation and the threat or use of force as means of settling international disputes.

In order to accomplish the aims of the preceding paragraph, land, sea, and air forces, as well as other war potential, will never be maintained. The right of belligerency of the state will not be recognized.

Because of Article 9, the paradoxical fact in Japan today is that Japanese who tend to be anti-American and to oppose American aims in the Far East also oppose any sort of constitutional revision lest this article too be revised. People who are pro-American and favor cooperation for mutual defense favor constitutional revision.

IT is ironic that the new Constitution went into effect in May 1947, only a few months before Secretary Royall announced the pending shift in policy. Since the shift, Article 9 has been a great source of embarrassment to American policy makers. It is not easy to justify even limited Japanese armament under the Constitution. The usual argument made is that the Constitution does not forbid arming for defense; but since people never admit to arming for anything but defense, one wonders why the controversial article was thought worth including in the first place. Really effective armament, moreover, will require some sort of conscription, which in turn will require constitutional amendment, and that is out of the question for the foreseeable future. Hence Americans must be reconciled to the fact that, by a certain lack of American foresight, the main burden of defending Japan will for an indefinite period continue to be American.

Back in 1946, when the Constitution was being drafted, there was another article that seemed even more controversial: Article 1, which demoted the emperor to "the symbol of the State and of the unity of the people, deriving his position from the will of the people with whom resides sovereign power." In the old Constitution he had been described as "combining in Himself the rights of sovereignty."

To conservatives this seemed a radical change indeed. In theory it most certainly was, for it cut the ground from under the most venerable of Japanese institutions, the exercising of power in the name of the emperor. The "revolution" passed quietly, however. Few people argue today that his majesty should be anything more than the symbol of the state.

Emperor Hirohito and his empress are popular, though not revered as emperors once were. Hirohito is a shy man whose public duties obviously make him uncomfortable and who would probably rather be down on the beach pursuing his hobby, marine biology. His consort is a dignified, maternal lady, whose presence does much to persuade the public that imperial family life is happy. It is testimony to their popularity that on January 2, 1961, more than 170,000 people trooped into the palace grounds to receive a wave of the symbolic hand. Significantly, however, those who had waited in line longest were from Yamagata Prefecture, one of the poorest, most backward areas in all Japan.

THE emperor receives more attention from the rural Japanese than from city dwellers. A young American was no doubt right when he said recently in *The New York Times* that his fellow students at a Japanese university were not interested in Crown Prince Akihito and his commoner bride. Shortly after the prince's wedding, when the popularity of the imperial house should have been at its highest, the Tokyo University student newspaper polled some five hundred students in four universities, and found that only about a third were in favor of leaving imperial arrangements as they were, whereas nearly half favored abolishing the monarchy.

If students notice the emperor at all, it is likely to be for purposes of criticizing him. Not many Americans would find much to object to, for example, in the emperor's New Year's poem for 1960:

This is my wish:
That the rays of the rising sun
May impartially light the corners of the world.

But the poem provoked a small controversy. Was his imperial majesty likening himself to the sun? an important university newspaper asked. And was he under the illusion that it was still his prerogative to do something about the welfare of the nation?

Whether or not the name of the emperor was sufficient in itself to send the Japanese off to war in 1941, it no longer seems sufficient to make them do much of anything. It has disappeared as the focus of or the ultimate sanction for power, and any attempt to restore its influence would meet with as much hostility as Queen Elizabeth II would if she arose one morning in London and announced that she meant to rule like Queen Elizabeth I.

HOW, then, have the people exercised their sovereignty since 1952, when the Occupation ended and they were for the first time in a position to exercise independent rule? One cannot say that they made a very promising start. Only three days after the San Francisco Treaty came into effect, restoring Japanese independence, there were bloody riots before the Imperial Palace, including attacks on American property. No violence of such proportions occurred again, however, until 1960, when a change in relations with the United States provoked a violent controversy. In the intervening years, Japanese politics were impressively stable. Time after time the electorate returned assemblies with comfortable pro-American majorities, or at least majorities committed to cooperating with the United States.

For some years now Japanese "renovationists"—by which term is meant everyone from the most moderate of non-revolutionary Socialists to Communists—have been worried over their inability to win more than about a third of the seats in the House of Representatives. With one third of the seats they are able to block constitutional amendment, but they are far from being able to legislate anything positive. Although the non-conservative vote has gone up in every lower-house election since 1952, while the vote of the conservatives has remained generally the same, the increase has not since 1953 been reflected in a proportionally greater number of Diet seats. Moreover, the growth of the non-conservative popular vote is leveling off, and, barring economic disaster, it will probably be a long time before the conservatives are voted out of power.

The fact is that the Japanese electorate is stable, even stolid, in its voting habits. Never was this more clearly demonstrated than in the 1960 elections. These were preceded by a year of violent political dissension, brought on by treaty negotiations with the United States. The Security Treaty which allied Japan and the United States and which went into effect in 1952 with the San Francisco Peace Treaty was revised by the two governments in 1960 to make Japan more nearly an equal partner. The duty of the United States to defend Japan, in return for Japanese cooperation, was made clear in a way it had not been in the 1952 treaty.

Some Japanese complain about specific provisions of the revised treaty, notably its failure to provide for a Japanese veto of proposed American troop movements. To emphasize such objections, however, is to miss the more important fact that the opposition was, and continues to be, not to the form of the treaty but to the treaty's very existence.

LATE in 1959 the opposition movement began resorting to violence. The Diet building was attacked by a radical student organization. Through the winter and spring of 1960 the resistance movement gathered momentum. Each "wave" (they were carefully numbered, lest the public forget what a determined movement it faced) was larger than the preceding one. In May the new treaty was finally ratified by the lower house of the Diet, and thereafter the violence increased in intensity, helped along no doubt by Prime Minister Kishi's unpopularity. Policemen were stoned, although in most democracies their handling of the mobs would have been thought restrained. Night after night, snake-dancing crowds took over the heart of the capital city. In June, a group of demonstrators tried to keep President Eisenhower's press secretary from entering the city. A few days later the most violent of the demonstrations led to the death of a girl student. Thereupon the proposed Eisenhower visit was canceled. In the course of the disturbances there were armed attacks upon two important politicians, one of them the prime minister, and a few months later came the assassination of the Socialist party chairman.

In brief, the year 1960 was a stormy time. Yet the events seem to have had almost no effect upon the elections of November 1960. In terms of seats in the House of Representatives, the ruling conservatives made fair gains over 1958, largely at the expense of independents. The non-conservatives stayed about where they were, although they did manage to elect candidates for the first time from certain highly conservative rural districts. The rise in the non-conservative vote was almost exactly equal to the rise in the total vote. Younger voters probably backed the non-conservative parties, but the chances are that almost no one else was induced to change his vote by the year's dramatic happenings. The events did not produce so much as a jog on the long-range curve.

SINCE the disappearance of General MacArthur, Japan has had no powerful political figure capable of moving the country, with the possible exception of Shigeru Yoshida, prime minister in 1946 and 1947, and again from 1948 to 1954. A tiny, peppery man, Yoshida looks a little like Churchill (a fondness for cigars perhaps contributes as much as anything to the impression), but he lacks the resonance of the Englishman. Confronted once by an offending photographer, he dashed a glass of water in the man's face. Long known as "One Man" (in English) for his refusal to admit the opinions of others, Yoshida is now the nearest thing the Japanese have to a much-loved elder statesman. Yet it would be impossible for him to come forward (like De Gaulle in France) and reunite a torn nation. For good or for bad, the great man has been lacking in post-treaty Japan.

Despite the outward stability and even the dullness of Japanese politics, violence is always lurking just out of sight beneath the calm, sunny surface. The Japanese are an emotional people, and a people who have traditionally put much faith in intuition. One cannot argue with people who are so intuitive and tell them to be reasonable. They will have their way—in acts of civic violence, which have beset the politics of Japan throughout its modern century; in a remarkable wishfulness, which we shall return to in a moment; and in a predilection for slogans that sometimes seem irrational. The slogan under which people rallied in May and June 1960 was *Ampo hantai* (Down with security).

THE most disturbing thing about Japan today is the polarization revealed by the unpleasantness of 1960. The two great forces in Japanese politics are far apart on matters of policy, especially foreign policy. On the one side is the Socialist opposition, and with it the larger part of the articulate intelligentsia. On the other side is the conservative government, and with it most of the people, who go along with the government's defense plans and with the American alliance either because they care little one way or the other or because they see no alternative.

When the Socialist party talks about domestic matters it does so in terms of a revolutionary Marxism that is rapidly becoming outmoded in Europe. The argument leaves a person wondering whether the parliamentary system would be permitted to remain in operation if the Socialists won power. When the party starts talking about foreign policy it begins to seem a bit wishful. It envisions a disarmed and neutral Japan, free from the entanglements of the American alliance and protected by a multilateral guarantee of Japanese neutrality—the guarantors including China and the Soviet Union.

Thus one may say that the Socialists of today have something ironically in common with the Occupation planners of 1945: in both cases, what is immediately distasteful and perhaps dangerous is allowed to overshadow more distant dangers and discomforts. The tables are turned, and to the Socialists the Security Treaty is what "Japanese militarism" was to Americans a decade and a half ago.

The present government, though conservative by comparison with the Socialists, is not reactionary. It is committed to vigorous economic expansion and, eventually, to something like the welfare state. In foreign policy it may be described as cautiously pessimistic, holding that China and the Soviet Union are not necessarily dangerous, but that the American alliance is advisable lest they prove to be so.

IT must be added, to complete the story, that there was a wider variety of "renovationist" or non-conservative parties in 1960 than in 1958. The Socialists split in late 1959, and in early 1960 a new party was formed, which called itself "Democratic Socialist" and which announced that it was in favor of ties with the West until such a time as world conditions permitted doing without them. This moderate position was rejected by the electorate. In the 1960 elections the new party was reduced to a minor faction. Therefore the polarization remains, and Japan today has a two-party system under which a change of regime would amount to a revolution, at least in foreign policy.

This statement of course assumes that the Socialists in power would be what they profess to be. But the Japanese are a paradoxical people, not to say a devious one, and never more so than when they set about drawing up party platforms; and it may be that the Socialists, if they eventually gain power, will prove less sanguine about Communism and less suspicious of the West than they now seem to be.

Judging by reports in the highbrow magazines and the big newspapers in Japan, the Socialist position has the support of the articulate intelligentsia. The Socialist party is ably abetted by the Communists, who are powerful in the labor unions, and the official policy of China and the Soviet Union now promotes Japanese "neutralism."

There are several possible explanations for what might be called the disaffection of the in-tellectuals from the western cause. Few of them, except those who are openly Communist, admit to being anti-western; and yet emotionalism, an insular ignorance of the world, a genuine desire for peace and an inability (or reluctance) to see an idea through to its consequences have driven them into a wishfulness about the East which automatically produces a fundamental hostility to the West. Some have probably been driven by fear or tempted into opportunism: they think they have seen the wave of the future, and they mean to ride it.

Perhaps the best explanation for the intelligentsia's attitude derives from the old Japanese tradition of importing finished systems. When the old Confucianism began to die around the time of World War I, Marxism came in as the best substitute, a new system for the old. Confucianism was a secular faith that purported to put this world in order and had little to say about other worlds, and Marxism does the same. As an all-encompassing theory Marxism has had no serious rival for the past 40 years except possibly the ultra-nationalism of the 1930s. But the ultra-nationalism was essentially a return to the discredited Confucianism in its emphasis on family-like relationships throughout society, and it had to be imposed by force.

THE thought control of the 1930s and 1940s, in addition to its other faults, did a disservice to the Japanese because it stopped the clock just when the great Soviet purges and the Hitler-Stalin pact were beginning to awaken and shock the peoples of many other countries. When the clock started again in 1945, the old assumptions of utopian Marxism were still there, unshaken by the cruelty and duplicity of Stalinism.

So things are today. The attack on the American alliance continues, and with it a campaign to undermine confidence in such basic institutions as the police and the courts. Sometimes one wonders how long the corrosion can go on. Yet the electorate remains stable, and there is no sign that anything short of a severe depression can seriously disturb the placid course of Japanese elections.

From the imperial box in Tokyo's Kōrakuen Stadium, Emperor Hirohito and his empress pleasantly acknowledge the greetings of 38,000

The Challenges of Transition

When Japan was put back on the road to liberal democracy following World War II, sovereignty was transferred from the emperor to the people. Today political power, once controlled by an oligarchy, is accessible to the masses, and the people are rising

baseball fans at a night game. The royal family, who lived in seclusion before the war, now make occasional appearances in public

to their opportunity. The country abounds in capable public servants. Their task of maintaining stable government, however, is complicated by the continuing threat of violence, which from time to time is stirred up by demagogues of the extreme Right or Left. These malcontents, who prey on the emotions of frustrated and impulsive students and other restive groups, are a reminder that a tradition of assassination has long plagued the course of Japanese politics.

ABOARD A TRAIN during his victorious 1960 campaign for election as prime minister, Ikeda (*opposite*) explains his pro-western views to a group of attentive newspapermen.

IN HIS GARDEN, Ikeda tends his favorite *bonsai* (miniature tree). He finds escape from the pressures of high office in the peace and quiet of his residence in Tokyo.

BOWING LOW (*left*), 29-year-old lawyer Kazuho Tani-kawa tries to hold the farm vote in his Hiroshima election district by responding to an old rice worker's obeisance.

SOAKING IN A TUB, Tanikawa (*above, center*) exchanges some election jokes with two farmer friends in a local doctor's private bath after a hard day of vote seeking around the neighborhood. Tanikawa's father, who held the same seat in the Diet, used to campaign in a frock coat. The son prefers more informal campaign methods.

VIOLENCE ERUPTS at a 1960 political meeting in Tokyo. The victim was Inejiro Asanuma, leader of the neutralist Socialist party, which bitterly opposed the Security Treaty with the U. S. The assassin, 17-year-old Otoya Yamaguchi, a right-wing fanatic, stabbed Asanuma to death with a foot-long samurai sword and later hanged himself in his cell in a house of detention.

ROYALTY *still commands the respect if not the reverence of the people*

DEVOTED SUBJECTS swarm over Nijūbashi Bridge into the Tokyo palace grounds to hail Emperor Hirohito on January 2, 1954. Sixteen were trampled to death in the crush.

HEIR APPARENT to one of the oldest monarchies in the world, Crown Prince Akihito (*opposite*) wears his robes of state at a ceremony in 1952 in honor of his 18th birthday.

A Resilient
and Growing
Economy

EVERY year, as a part of its annual review of
living conditions in Japan, the prime minister's office provides a portrait of a "typical"
Japanese urban family—the Nakamuras, let us
call them. The prime minister has told us something about the Nakamuras: they have two
growing children, Mr. Nakamura is the only
wage earner in the family, and they are a sort of
composite of all urban working or white-collar
families in the country.

Given this much, we may imagine a number
of other things. Since Mr. Nakamura stands
somewhere near the line where the better-paid
laboring class merges into the white-collar class,
he cannot afford much waste. Yet he and Mrs.
Nakamura and the two small ones manage to
look neat and not too far out of the mode. Mr.
Nakamura owns an acceptable business suit or
two and several kimonos, appropriate to the
season, to change into when he gets home

from work. Mrs. Nakamura very likely wears western clothes that lag some distance behind Paris (the Japanese kimono, she will tell you, is expensive, time-consuming and uncomfortable). Young Master Nakamura is usually turned out in a brass-buttoned student uniform, young Miss Nakamura in the middy blouse that is the feminine equivalent.

TO be presentable outside the house, the Nakamuras are likely to make sacrifices at home. They will occupy perhaps two sparsely furnished rooms, whose badly tended floor mats invite drafts and, unless the annual cleaning is thorough, vermin. For entertainment, a movie every other week or so and an occasional trip to the zoo suffice—plus whatever Mr. Nakamura is able to arrange through his business. The trip to the zoo requires a camera, for the children must be snapped in front of the elephant cage, and it may also require a transistor radio. The camera and the transistor radio are among the great Japanese luxuries.

In short, the Nakamuras manage to look not very different from middle-class people everywhere, and even to indulge a modest craving for luxuries; but the hard fact is that their budget is kept precariously in balance only by rigid self-denial. Much the same thing can be said of the national budget of Japan. Just as Mr. Nakamura cannot very often surrender to the lure of a few after-work drinks downtown without throwing his accounts out of balance, so the country can allow itself certain luxuries, but has to be careful.

Between January and November 1959, according to the prime minister's figures, Mr. Nakamura had to get by each month with an average of ¥37,905, or just over $105 at the official exchange rate of 360 yen to the dollar. During the month the Nakamuras virtually demolished the $105, but they still ended up with a little more than they had had at the beginning (*see box*).

Mr. Nakamura's monthly pay envelope and the spending of it tell only part of the story, however. Because there is very little slack in the

A FAMILY'S MONTHLY BUDGET

HOUSING AND UTILITIES		
Rent	$1.95	
Utilities and Other Costs	8.81	10.76
CLOTHING AND PERSONAL EFFECTS		8.14
FOOD		
Rice and Other Cereals	8.23	
Meat and Fish	4.73	
Fruits and Vegetables	3.98	
Milk and Eggs	2.38	
Alcoholic Beverages	1.17	
Other Foods	9.06	29.55
MISCELLANEOUS LIVING EXPENSES		
Reading and Recreation	4.87	
Social Expenses	3.67	
Personal Grooming	2.45	
Education	2.02	
Medical Care	1.89	
Transportation and Communications	1.61	
Other	8.18	24.69
TAXES AND SOCIAL SECURITY		7.11
MISCELLANEOUS EXPENDITURES		
Savings	3.22	
Insurance Premiums	4.13	
Installment Payments	5.40	
Debt Payments	10.57	
Other	1.56	24.88
TOTAL EXPENDITURES		**$105.13**
MONTHLY INCOME		**$105.29**

NARROW MARGIN of income over expenditures for an average Japanese family is shown above. "Personal grooming" includes barber and beauty shop charges. The low cost of goods and services in Japan is reflected in such items as medical care. Typical doctor's charges are 50 cents for an office call, $11.11 for an appendectomy.

budget, any kind of emergency or special expense will throw it hopelessly out of balance. What keeps the Nakamuras going—and enables them to buy luxuries like transistor radios—is the semiannual bonus. Every wage earner expects these payments, which are usually made in June and December. The December bonus generally comes to some two or three months' wages. If Mr. Nakamura's employer were suddenly to cancel the company bonus program, the Nakamura family budget would be severely strained. Mr. Nakamura lives beyond his immediate monthly means in confidence that December and June will bring boosts.

Yet he cannot be said to indulge himself excessively. His typical meal is chiefly rice, and rice that has had most of its vitamin content polished away. The average Japanese diet is heavily weighted with starch, and the balanced meal is not common to it. The average worker or salary earner is almost puritanical, it would seem, when it comes to alcohol. His monthly expenditures allow him but a swallow or so of the cheapest *saké* (rice wine) daily.

BUT most striking is the way he scrimps on housing. The cramped Nakamura rooms are separated by paper doors, inadequate to keep the softest remark from becoming family property. The crowding is mitigated somewhat, however, by the fact that the typical Japanese room is all-purpose, and so uncluttered with objects that people can occupy most of it. At night the table is pushed to one side and bedding spread on the straw mats; during the day the bedding goes into a closet and the table comes back to the center. In the winter the table even serves as part of a heating unit, acting as a cover for a small pit of hot coals that warm the hands and feet. The looseness of Japanese construction allows the wind to whistle through the cracks and makes heating an entire house almost out of the question; and so, for warmth, a person must apply himself to this one spot. A brazier or a gas or electric plate suffices for cooking.

For certain other things, however, the Nakamura family spends its money fairly liberally. More goes for personal grooming (the barber and the beauty shop) in a month than goes for rent. More is spent on clothing than on almost any other single item in the budget, and nearly three times as much goes for clothing as for rent.

One may conclude, then, that most Japanese economize rigidly on food and housing and indulge a modest craving for luxuries elsewhere. Yet something of a mystery remains. Mr. Nakamura, observed on a commuter's train, seems better groomed than his budget would lead one to expect. The average Tokyo commuter is at least as well dressed as the average person on a New York subway train. Especially in the cities, class distinctions seem to disappear when people

dress up for an evening on the town. The delivery boy on his day off looks very much like the rich boy from business school. It would seem that something must have been left out of the typical family's accounts.

Partly it is what might be called fringe benefits. Housing expenses for many families are low because the company often provides housing, and a company may even provide clothes for a workman, though not for his wife and children. Even so a person wonders: Are there statistics which no one could possibly allow the prime minister's investigators to come upon? Expense accounts provide one possible answer. An office worker with enough rank can allow himself a fondness for geisha parties without having them show on the family budget.

There are other irregular practices as well, and the possibilities for indulging in them rise with a person's income. An employee does not always put his company's interests first when he sees a chance of lining his own pockets. The idea of a gift in return for a favor is so much a part of Japanese life that a person whose approval is required for a contract is quite likely to ask the other party in the negotiations for a washing machine or an electric fan, and if the contract is important the latter will generally oblige. The institution of the kickback reaches to the highest levels of Japanese business.

But here one enters the realm of speculation, and can only marvel that the urban Japanese dresses and plays as liberally as he does. The fascinating problem of the family budget remains to be fully explored.

IT must be remembered that Mr. Nakamura is a city dweller. He does better than his country cousin. In August 1960 nine out of 10 urban Japanese households had a radio, more than half had a television set and almost half had an electric fan and an electric washing machine. The farmer was not so well off. In February of the same year, farm households had as many radios as urban ones, but only one farm family in nine had a television set, and still fewer had fans and washing machines.

There are other gloomy spots in the economy, but housing is the gloomiest. The Construction Ministry estimated that the shortage of houses in 1959 ran to a total of 2.4 million, and had fallen by less than half a million since 1955. Two households out of every three were occupied by more than a person and a half per room.

The Japanese people's fondness for crowds is well known, but as far as housing is concerned most of them have little choice in the matter. The cold statistics come abruptly to life when a person picks up his morning paper and sees that another child has been smothered to death by the half dozen brothers and sisters he was sleeping with, or that another fire has wiped out a platoon or so of employees asleep in the attic of some shop. Not long ago four young men died when a small Tokyo cleaning plant burned down, but the toll was small compared to what it might have been. Eleven men had been sleeping in a second-floor room about four yards square, and five women had been sleeping next door in a room about half that size.

There are many inequalities in the distribution of the national income. The Ministry of Welfare has assembled statistics showing that the urban consumer, who is already ahead of his rural counterpart, is moving farther ahead. The same is true of the office worker as compared with the manual laborer, and of the better-off laborer as compared with those who must receive public assistance.

YET despite inequalities and inadequacies, all classes in Japan today are moving ahead in varying degrees, and the number of people on relief grows smaller every year. The problem of overcoming inequalities would therefore seem to be less important than the problem of the country's general economic growth. If Mr. Nakamura's economic situation is on the whole encouraging, so is that of his country.

In the single year 1959 the gross national product rose by about a sixth, or three times the rate for West Germany, and exports rose by a quarter, or over twice the German rate. This high rate is partly caused by the fact that the base from which the rise was recorded was smaller in Japan, so that each unit of absolute increase was proportionately greater. But it was nonetheless a most substantial achievement. Per capita income in 1959 was one and a half times the prewar level.

Japanese economic growth is not of the sort that shows itself in guided missiles rather than in ordinary comforts. The list of the biggest money-making Japanese corporations in 1959 is headed by the Bank of Japan, but the next three are all makers of electronic equipment—and the electronics industry exists largely for the consumer. One should not think, however, that these luxuries are throwing the nation's accounts out of balance, any more than Mr. Nakamura's purchase of a camera ruins his household budget. The balance of international payments has been generally favorable to Japan, and in recent years the country's foreign exchange reserves have risen sharply. To a country that must live by exports, this is a heartening development. Moreover, the nature of foreign trade is changing, and changing in a way to suggest that the country will not be caught unprepared when inevitably it loses its position as the great exploiter of cheap labor.

BEFORE the war, Japan made its way by concentrating a large supply of labor on light industries, but the day when "made in Japan" meant that a product was shoddy and produced in a sweatshop has passed. And new markets are replacing old ones. Europe, which in the mid-1930s took only 8 per cent of Japanese exports, took 12 per cent in the first half of 1960, and the percentage taken by North America almost doubled in the same period, from 18 to 35 per cent. The ability of the Japanese to move on to producing something else as less advanced countries take over their traditional functions and markets was demonstrated in 1959, when Japanese exports of electronics tripled.

The future of this resilient economy is controversial. Everyone expects it to go on growing, unless there is a really serious recession in the United States, and the big question is how

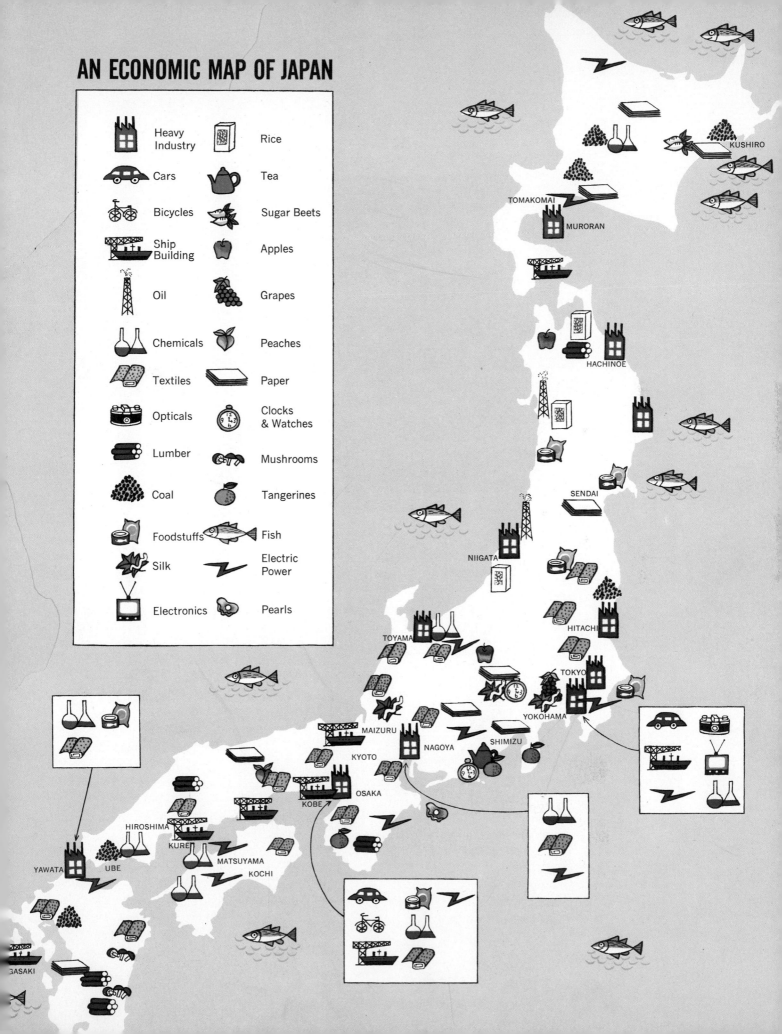

AN ECONOMIC MAP OF JAPAN

Legend:

Symbol	Meaning	Symbol	Meaning
	Heavy Industry		Rice
	Cars		Tea
	Bicycles		Sugar Beets
	Ship Building		Apples
	Oil		Grapes
	Chemicals		Peaches
	Textiles		Paper
	Opticals		Clocks & Watches
	Lumber		Mushrooms
	Coal		Tangerines
	Foodstuffs		Fish
	Silk		Electric Power
	Electronics		Pearls

Place names:

KUSHIRO
TOMAKOMAI
MURORAN
HACHINOE
SENDAI
NIIGATA
HITACHI
TOYAMA
TOKYO
YOKOHAMA
MAIZURU
NAGOYA
SHIMIZU
KYOTO
OSAKA
KOBE
HIROSHIMA
KURE
MATSUYAMA
KOCHI
YAWATA
UBE
GASAKI

fast it will grow. The conservative party naturally takes a sunnier view than the Socialist opposition. The government's economic advisers believe that the national income can be doubled in 10 years. To this, economists generally associated with the Socialist party reply with a number of arguments. First of all, they say that changes in the international market are likely to slow down exports. Secondly, they hold that the completion of war rehabilitation will bring a similar slowdown at home.

A third criticism of the optimistic official view is worth some attention, because it leads to a consideration of the "dual structure" of the Japanese economy, one of its most curious characteristics. Socialist economists argue that economic growth will lead to further inequalities of wealth. Whether or not they are right depends largely on whether or not the dual structure continues. It is necessary to look at this last in some detail.

JAPANESE industry is divided into two sorts of companies. One kind is the large modernized company which, because of a big outlay for advanced techniques, has succeeded in greatly increasing the productivity of its labor force. The other is a more traditional sort of firm, the small one that has little capital outlay and, in sweatshop fashion, relies on cheap labor to make its products competitive. The question of whether or not inequalities will continue in the Japanese economy depends in large measure on whether or not companies of the second sort are able to survive as the economy grows. Will the overworked laborer in the small plant—the lower half of the dual economy—awaken to his opportunities and push his way into the other half, thereby leaving his former employer with an insuperable labor problem?

The question is complicated by the fact that often the two kinds of companies are interlocked. The most modern industrial establishments frequently let out contracts to cottage industries. Visiting some remote spot where folk pottery survives, one is quite likely to come upon rows of inartistic pluglike objects drying

in the sun, and to learn that they are part of an order from one of the biggest electronics makers in the land. The rural potter can supply the huge Hitachi enterprises because labor costs are minimal and he needs almost no capital.

The existence of the dual structure makes it impossible to talk about "the working class" in Japan. There are two working classes: the organized elite, employed by advanced, highly mechanized concerns; and workers for small enterprises, unorganized and underpaid in comparison to the elite. Strikes are almost always staged by organized groups, whose way of life must seem like one long, well-paid picnic to the unorganized worker in the small plant.

Although most large companies do better by their workers than do the small companies, they have generally invited suspicion as representing too heavy a concentration of power. Furthermore, certain of the great industrial combines played a sinister part in Japan's prewar military adventuring. It was therefore the top half of the dual structure that the American Occupation in 1945 set about dispersing and "deconcentrating." The initial post-surrender statement of policy announced this as one of the economic aims of the Occupation: "To favor a program for the dissolution of the large industrial and banking combinations which have exercised control of a great part of Japan's trade and industry." Major holding companies of the sort that had allied themselves with undemocratic elements before the war were dissolved, and holdings by one company of a sister company's stock were prohibited.

EVEN before the Occupation ended, the retreat from the deconcentration measures had begun. Partly this was because no important group in Japanese society had benefited directly from the program, and partly because the emphasis of Occupation policies had shifted away from reform and in the direction of recovery. Today the attempt at deconcentration can be considered a total failure. The old combines are pretty well together again, though in somewhat different form. Exchanges of stock among member companies are no longer illegal. But the real center of economic power today, corresponding to the old holding company, is the bank of the industrial and financial combine.

Combines are held together not only by the banks but by their huge trading companies, which act as marketing agencies for the combines as units, and by informal associations among their executives, who continue to think of themselves as members of the same family. Thus the heads of the firms once owned by Mitsui, largest of the old combines, have an informal social organization called the Monday Club.

THE big companies treat their employees in a paternalistic fashion that sometimes approaches the Marxian ideal of payment not according to services rendered but according to need. Family benefits are common, so that the worker with a family receives more than an unmarried fellow worker on the same job. Fringe benefits are elaborate, frequently including medical services and hospitalization, and generally including pensions. Sometimes the benefits more than double the nominal wage.

Hours of work in the big companies are long by American standards, but not by the standards of the Japanese farm or small business. Wages are not impressive by American standards, but they are considerably higher in the large firms. In 1959 the average worker for a company employing five to 29 people received only half the wages of the worker for a company with more than 500 employees.

It is because of such facts that the small entrepreneur in the lower half of the dual structure will have problems as the economy grows. His supply of cheap labor is likely to dwindle, and with it will go his ability to compete. His employees will be in a hurry to move into the better-paid upper half.

Working for a big company can seem very comforting. A modern electronics plant is likely to be antiseptically clean and well lighted. Indeed, it bears a strong resemblance to a hospital laboratory. The white-garbed transistor technicians might well be analyzing cardiograms or preparing for surgery, so germ-free do the surroundings seem. Many of the workers are even equipped with masks, for lung ailments are common and the Japanese, much in fear of them, derive great comfort from masks.

Beyond the broad windows the company lawn looks pleasant and inviting. On the roof there are volleyball courts and ping-pong tables for those who wish to spend the noon hour competitively, and medicine balls for those who do not. There are likely to be company dormitories, and the personnel are able to choose from a wide variety of social and educational "circles," where they exchange magazines, discuss striking for more ping-pong tables, or join in singing "Old Black Joe" and other songs.

In short, the big firms provide protection from the winds that blow, and this is responsible for the great contradiction in the Japanese labor movement. The strongest unions are led by doctrinaire Marxists, but surveys show that the members of these unions are quite un-Marxian in their tastes and ambitions.

THE boy who comes off the farm and goes to work for a small establishment, on the other hand, can expect to rise at dawn and work until after nightfall with no more than two days off a month. The shop will be dark and dingy, and there will be no fringe benefits save what the employer feels duty-bound to provide. Yet the wages of even the lowest-paid workers are rising, and the bright electronics and camera factories are beckoning.

As the economy grows, and the farm boy who has been willing to work near his home and make electronics plugs goes to work for the big electronics plant over the hill, labor costs will become an item that can no longer be ignored, and so the dual structure may be expected to disappear. The change will not be painless. The young people will be no problem, for they are mobile and will no doubt be pleased at the shorter hours and better pay they have at the electronics plant. For the middle-aged and older people, the transition will be difficult, for it will mean the loss of a cherished independence.

Widening Gap in Ways of Living and Working

"Japan is a world the reverse of Europe. Hardly in anything do their ways conform to ours. They eat and dress . . . differently. . . . Their methods of doing business, their manner of sitting down, their buildings, their domestic arrangements . . . are so unlike ours as to be beyond description or understanding." The astonished voyager was Father Alexandro Valignano, an Italian Jesuit who four centuries ago followed St. Francis Xavier to Japan as a fisher of souls. Valignano would be puzzled today by contrasts between the medieval cottage economy he saw then, which has persisted until the present time in the countryside, and the modern industrialism that lives side by side with it. The "dual structure" of the modern Japanese economy is also reflected in contrasting standards of living. Although there has been a sharp upward trend in general living conditions for all classes, the gap between town and country, between unskilled labor and organized factory workers continues to widen at an accelerating speed.

PULLING UP SEEDLINGS of rice in rich paddies near Lake Suwa, women transplant the sprouts to fields cleared of the stubble of winter wheat. Rice is Japan's staple diet.

GATHERING FOR SUPPER, a farm family sits around an open *irori* fireplace with its traditional iron kettle. Their food consists of soup with noodles, rice and tea. It is cooked and served by the farmer's daughter-in-law, who by ancient custom is a maid of all work. The men are still in work clothes after a long day in the fields.

ARRIVING HOME, Akio Hasegawa, who owns a kimono store in Kyoto, puts aside his business suit and is helped into a kimono by his wife on the veranda of his home.

CHOOSING A SCROLL, or *kakemono*, from his collection (*left*), Akio will hang it for a month in the *tokonoma*, or alcove of honor, the most revered corner of the home.

PLAYING CARDS makes an amusing evening. Here three generations of the Hasegawa family play "One Hundred Poems." Grandfather Daisaburo (*center*) makes them roar with laughter by chanting the first half of a classical poem in the style of a monk, while his children and grandchildren hunt for the matching half on cards on the floor.

71

THE BOUNTIFUL SEA *is a major source of work and sustenance for a people seldom out of sight of its shores*

TWIN TANKERS (*opposite*) are built simultaneously at a Kure shipyard. Each weighs 85,000 tons, but leviathans of 125,000 tons are now under construction.

FISHING FLEET (*right*) is made ready for the harvest by the seagoing villagers of Enoshima. Japan has nearly 400,000 fishing boats in service off its shores.

HEAVY CATCHES (*below*) are made close inshore by dredging, often done by women. Among the most popular fish are bream, mackerel, flounder and mullet.

PRECISION *and a*
painstaking care for detail
give Japanese workmanship great
renown in a world eager
for the products of its skill

DEFT HANDS in the Kosuge factory (*left*) use Detroit methods to make toy cars. Once known for cheap construction, Japanese production is now famed for quality.

KEEN EYES of transistor workers at the spotless, efficient Sony factory in Tokyo concentrate on the delicate job of piecing together small radio sets and tape recorders. Some 3,000 employees here make an average of 120,000 radios and 13,000 tape machines monthly. The electronics industry produces 5 per cent of Japan's exports.

Catering to the craze for American popular music which has seized the youth of Japan, rock-a-billy vocalist Masaaki Hirao, son of a

cosmetic manufacturer, belts out numbers for a receptive audience

5

Upheavals in Family and Society

THE defeat of 1945 shook Japanese society profoundly, bringing changes and dislocations whose effects are still being felt. Although the 1945 debacle is often compared with the abrupt reversals that occurred in 1867 and 1868, when the Tokugawa shogunate was overthrown and the West came flooding in, the repercussions of 1945 were far deeper. The World War II defeat marked the end of something basic, for the principles of loyalty and duty which were the core of Japanese life and custom were challenged as they had not been in 1867.

To understand those principles it is necessary to recall the essential thoughtlessness of Japanese thought. The technician, the commentator, the weigher and measurer of natural objects are common enough in Japanese history, but the creator of bold, rational systems is rare. The two main traditions of medieval Japanese Buddhism (that is, of Buddhism between about 1200 and about 1600) were both fundamentally anti-rational. One was a simple pietism, the

77

religion of the masses, which preached complete surrender to the saving power of the lord Amida. The other was the more aristocratic Zen tradition, which had a profound influence on the arts and was the reverse of popular Buddhism in urging action and self-cultivation, but which was at one with it in ultimately denying the power of the intellect. Indeed, the denial by Zen has traditionally been the more aggressive of the two. A person does not make generalizations about Zen, including the generalization that has just been made, unless he is resigned to being beaten about the head and shoulders by some Zen master, who will come up roaring: "Zen is not words!"

It was upon this intuitive way of the mind that the Tokugawa shoguns (in power from the 17th Century to the mid-19th) set about imposing a conformity so absolute that it might better be described as blind identification: identification with one's group and one's betters, and with the state through the father of the family and the fatherlike leader of the clique or faction. They succeeded remarkably well. When the modern Canadian historian E. H. Norman set out in a search through Japanese literature to locate a critic of Tokugawa society and a "stalwart champion who stood forth to break a lance against despotism," he found only "pale and insubstantial shadows." Finally, in a last effort, he unearthed Andō Shōeki, an obscure rustic thinker who lived around 1700 and whom most Japanese had never heard of.

WHEN the great changes of 1867 and 1868 occurred, it was a relatively simple matter for the ultimate object of identification to become the young Emperor Meiji, and the Meiji success story began. In 1945 such a transfer of loyalty was far more difficult because the leaders of the country were discredited and no longer worthy to be objects of identification. The object of reverence and loyalty, the father of the family and state, had, in effect, died. For many Japanese, of course, he had died long before, and had been replaced by new gods, whose attributes were largely "scientific"—the

"scientific" historiography of Marx, the positivism of the natural sciences and so on. For others, the 1945 shock brought deprivation. Some of them, particularly on the farms, continued to be in the grip of family authority, but this domination was not as easily taken for granted as it had once been. One discontented young man from a rural area said recently in a newspaper interview, "It's a pretty dismal thing, being the oldest son of a farmer. You're tied to the family, you're driven out into the fields, and you don't have time or money for any fun."

AS the young fellow's remarks suggest, the old family system is still strong outside the cities. The father is a tyrant against whom a son must be very intrepid indeed to rebel, and the oldest son, who can expect to inherit the whole of the family property even though the American Occupation tried to end primogeniture, has the other sons and daughters quite at his mercy. In the urban areas, however, the old system is breaking down.

The rising young urban generation has set about turning the old principles upside down. The vogue is to emphasize parental duties, where it once was to stress filial duties. When some 16-year-old boy butchers a girl student (this happens from time to time) the newspapers can generally be counted on to call in child psychologists who will point out that it was not really the boy's fault, for he was reared in an insufficiently loving atmosphere.

The old relationship between mother-in-law and daughter-in-law is also being reversed. It used to be the case, and it frequently still is in the country, that the mother-in-law was a tyrant and the daughter-in-law could not expect her own husband to protect her from the older woman's vindictiveness. A writer of an advice-to-the-troubled column for a large newspaper recently remarked, however, that her sympathies were shifting to the side of the mother-in-law. According to the columnist, there are households in which the poor woman cannot open her mouth without being accused of undemocratic, old-fashioned views.

Yet the "leveling process" has not brought about free association among family members as equals. If anything, it has introduced an element of uneasiness, and so increased the stiffness. Meanwhile the oldest brother continues to be reared differently from the other brothers, and the brothers from the sisters, and so everyone knows his place—if only to rebel against it. The father is an aloof figure who never thinks of telephoning when he will not be home for dinner. He no longer brings home the children of his extramarital affairs for his wife to rear, as he once did, but the evidence in the newspapers is that he still considers it his privilege to have the affairs. The mother envelops her children in animal warmth during their earliest years, but when their needs start becoming more subtle she has little to say to them.

INDEED there can be few countries where communication between the generations is breaking down at a more rapid rate. Partly this is a matter of language. The father is usually able to read a sort of prose, still strongly under the influence of the Chinese classics, that is too much trouble for his son. Meanwhile the son has acquired a strange language influenced by Marx and Hollywood that is often gibberish to his father.

Education, too, has changed. Even if the father is one of those who long ago found new gods for the old ones, he is still a product of traditional education, with its emphasis on knowing one's place, and in whatever tight little faction he belongs, in business or cultural affairs, subordination is probably still the rule. The son will one day have his own faction, no doubt, but thus far everything that his "progressive" teachers have taught him makes his father's ways look so feudal that he sees no point in talking.

Yet the child psychologist who upbraids parents for having failed to provide a sufficiently loving atmosphere and the teacher or professor who says "feudal" things are the greatest evils are not likely themselves to be models of ideal behavior. Rather they are likely to be aloof and

chilly, and nowhere is factionalism as rampant as in the academic world. It is indicative of the state of things, to cite a small example, that the inter-library loan is practically unknown in Japan. When one university learns that it has a book not present at another university the impulse is not to offer the book but to lock it up.

In this fragmented world, it is not at all surprising that the student should turn up in the singing tearooms which are so widespread in Tokyo today. There he can at least sing belligerently peaceful songs with other self-appointed victims of future nuclear wars. But some of his reactions are far more alarming. A complete rejection of authority is one symptom—a belief that anything goes. Extreme, unbridled individualism is one of the themes running through postwar Japanese literature. In a novel by Ooka published in 1950, the young hero meditates on the state of man and the world: "The chaos of defeat strengthened the idea that had been in his heart, as a stepchild, from long before: that he had only himself to rely on. . . . The behavior of the Japanese people after his release from the army merely underwrote the conviction. He had no interest in the student movement, he did not believe in democracy."

BUT perhaps the supreme exponent of such ethics (or lack of ethics) was a young student named Kōji Yamazaki who in the years just after the war came into some prominence as a seemingly successful speculator. One of his mottoes, it seems, was: "If you don't rape her, someone else will." Although he seemed to be making tremendous amounts of money, young Yamazaki presently found himself unable to pay his debts. He thereupon committed suicide—evidently to atone for violating the one principle he allowed himself, the sanctity of the contract.

Another manifestation of the postwar malaise is the incidence of crime and suicide. Japanese suicide is a highly complicated phenomenon. Sometimes it seems to be nothing new at all but a remarkable survival of something very old. Such was the case with the young right-wing fanatic who in 1960 assassinated the chairman of the Socialist party and then killed himself. His compulsion was evidently a holdover from the blind identification with father and group that characterized Tokugawa Japan. Sometimes suicide can be a somewhat theatrical gesture, the romantic climax to a romantic career, as when the flamboyant, aggressively profligate novelist Osamu Dazai drowned himself in 1948. (Even now, however, there lingers a suspicion that his girl friend pushed him in.)

Finally, suicide often seems to embody an afterglow of pietist Buddhism, as witnessed by the extraordinary incidence of double suicides, in which lovers kept apart in this world travel together to the next. In any event, there is no escaping the significant fact that Japan has by far the highest rate in the world for suicides by young people. Suicide is the largest single cause of death in Japan among young people between the ages of 15 and 24.

AS in many other countries, juvenile delinquency is rising rapidly, and the age of the delinquents is falling. In one year, 1959, transgressions by people under 16 rose by nearly a quarter, while the figure for minors in general was rising by a little more than a tenth. The nature of the crimes is also changing. Those of a violent nature are rising rapidly, and sex crimes the most rapidly of all. Of this last fact, however, the Japanese Ministry of Health and Welfare is able to take a surprisingly sunny view: it suggests that young people are healthier (certainly they are much larger than they used to be) and hence have more wild oats to sow.

It is hard to see, however, why the young people must resort to crime in their search for gratification, unless, like well-fed cats hunting sparrows, it is the taking and not the taken that interests them. Nowhere in the world is gratification easier to come by than in a large Japanese city, particularly Tokyo. The dress of the young is extravagantly provocative, being derived from Hollywood, and once provoked they have all manner of crannies to withdraw to: cheap inns that ask no questions and rent rooms

by the hour; bars to please everyone from Narcissus to satyr; dance halls where it is too crowded to do anything but jostle and snuggle; dark coffee shops where almost anything can happen; dark movie theaters where everything short of "the final line" is crossed; Turkish baths that have leaped in to fill the gap left by the outlawing of prostitution in 1958; and brothels that thrive under many other names. Tokyo is a great pot of flesh. Foreign visitors are sometimes reminded of the Berlin of the Weimar Republic.

YET in spite of all these disturbing signs, fragmentation may yet be the salvation of democratic Japan. It seems to operate universally, on the enemies of democracy as much as on everyone else. The demonstrations against the Japanese-American Security Treaty in May and June 1960 would have been far more dangerous if they had been part of a united movement. Instead they were made up of badly assorted fragments, rather like the pieces of several jigsaw puzzles mixed up in one box. The demonstrators banded together because of a vague fear of foreign entanglements and because of a strangely festive atmosphere, and presently they began quarreling among themselves. Almost the last act of violence came when the left-wing Zengakuren students' union attacked the headquarters of the Communist party. The latter retaliated by denouncing the Zengakuren as a hireling of American imperialism.

In addition to being at odds with each other, the Zengakuren and the Communists are both at odds internally. The Zengakuren is badly split, with each wing calling itself the true custodian of the Marxist heritage, and the Communist party is similarly faction-ridden. Unless outside forces intervene, it is possible that the fragments of May and June 1960 will not come together again.

One sometimes wonders if the crowds of pleasure seekers are happy. There is something frantic about them, milling around, all feet and elbows, pushing their way off trains so that other crowds can push their way on, forming lines a hundred yards long to board trains that will take them to the mountains, where they can push one another off cliffs and poke skis in one another's eyes. On a single mountain northwest of Tokyo more than 30 people fell over cliffs in 1959 and again in 1960. During the last week of December 1960, the National Railways provided transportation for half the population of the land. While the Japanese movie industry is not particularly worried about the competition offered by television, it does fear that the enormous vogue for travel will cut into the box office as more people can afford to go on excursions.

They are very restless, these people on the move, and prepared to face the rigors of cheap travel—a taxing, arduous business—just for the sake of getting somewhere. The rotunda of Tokyo Central Station at six o'clock any evening resembles a heating pan of popcorn, and in Shinjuku and Ueno Stations, where people catch the ski trains, the effect is intensified by the fact that the pan is not large enough. So one asks the question: Are they happy? Might they not be happier if some strong man were to come along and tell them to sit down for a while, to stop buzzing, to be done with this frantic pursuit of pleasure?

FOR there is another side to the story. In spite of such exaggerated individualists as Ooka's hero and young Yamazaki, the Japanese may still be called a docile people, and a people with a strong urge to conform. Today, just as in the period explored by E. H. Norman, the true rebel is not easy to find.

Tokyo may be a huge fleshpot and juvenile delinquency may be on the rise, but these facts are inconclusive. Japanese equivalents of the Kinsey Report suggest that there is still a powerful strain of propriety among all classes. Although the reports are often wildly unscientific, they agree that sexual experimentation is considerably rarer among young Japanese than Kinsey found it to be among young Americans.

Under certain circumstances where one might expect violence, the Japanese show a surprising docility. An American psychiatrist on a visit to Japan once described his astonishment at seeing the most explosive sort of psychotic patients separated from each other only by a pane of glass. And Japanese drunks are among the most amiable in the world. Where the Irish drunk might be expected to grow belligerent, the Japanese drunk grows talkative, sentimental and affectionate. Perhaps he has been so trained to follow social forms from childhood that he follows them even when he has temporarily lost control of his faculties.

SO one is driven to the conclusion that the Japanese are a people with a strong urge to conform, although today they have little to conform to except fads, ceremonial traditions and a vague mood. On an intellectual level the mood is the anti-western one which brought the demonstrators of 1960 together. Emotionally it finds expression in the restless moving about through the country and from one fad to another. In this highly fragmented society a great many people feel that they belong to nothing at all. The transition to totalitarianism would be less painful for the Japanese than for any western people. Indeed one wonders, watching them jump restlessly about, if such a change would not make them happier.

Occasionally a few of them do go off to Red China, and almost everyone who does comes back wearing a dazed smile, and sits down to write his anthem of praise to Chairman Mao. Here, for instance, writing in the Peking monthly *Chinese Literature*, is Miss Yōko Matsuoka, who was educated in the U.S. and is known internationally for her autobiography: "If you had listened with closed eyes, in other words, if you had not known that it was Chairman Mao speaking, the unassuming tone of his conversation would lead you to think that you were listening to a favorite uncle rather than the great leader of the nation. We all had this sense of intimacy in Chairman Mao's presence, all felt as if enveloped in the warmth of that great heart."

A person is tempted to suspect that the dead father of the Tokugawa family and state may have been born again.

Youth's Quest for a New Identity

ON A TOKYO STREET, a young couple stroll together after nightfall. The younger generation can now enjoy the pleasures of dating, which were forbidden to their parents.

AT A UNIVERSITY DANCE (*right*), girls in kimonos and in western clothes chat informally with their escorts. But strict decorum is observed and the dance ends at 9:30 p.m.

The urban youth of Japan are heavily engaged in the search for new values to replace old dogmas in which they have no confidence. It is a process prickly for themselves and painful to their elders, who still submissively accept the authority of family, religion and state that is so brusquely rejected by their restless children. Sometimes the quest of youth ends bleakly in a withdrawal into self, but more often it ends in the excitement of new ideas and new heroes.

PEACEFUL PROTEST in song (*opposite*) to drive away the A-bomb and other nightmares is made nightly by young patrons of Tomoshibi, a famous Tokyo singing tearoom.

VEHEMENT PROTEST is organized by the Zengakuren students' group, whose agitators, Kentarō Karōji (*left*), Takeo Shimizu and Kōichirō Shino, led rioting in 1959.

TEENAGERS' IDOL, movie star Reiko Dan (*left*), 24, is a leader of the gilded youth in Japan whose life of American-style luxury attracts widespread envy.

RICH REWARDS of movie fame for Fujiko Yamamoto (*opposite, right*) include $100,000 a year and a $90,000 villa, which she enjoys with her mother.

Reflections in the placid water are cast by trees and stonework in the classical garden laid out 350 years ago by Kobori Enshū around the

Traces of Spirit

Katsura Imperial Villa in Kyoto. Here a marriage of human artifice and natural loveliness creates a feeling of tranquillity and harmony

FOR the finer manifestations of "the Japanese spirit"—that hardy native essence which throughout history has made the country's borrowing from other lands something more than simple imitation—the inquiring outsider should look to the arts of Japan. If he is lucky enough to be in Japan while he is making his inquiries, he should note the sensitive awareness of nature that forms the basis of the arts, and somehow manages to withstand the onslaughts of modernization. In architecture, painting, the dramatic arts and certain forms of literature, the Japanese contribution has been so original that anyone who has recognized it is the richer for having done so.

In the preceding chapters the emphasis has been on change, and this may have given the impression of a nation racing madly away from its past, eager to be done with the whole fusty business. Yet for all the change, there remains within the Japanese a stubborn cultural conservatism. Just as a millennium ago that rock of native spirit reared above the flood of borrowing from the Chinese, so today a distinctly

Japanese feeling for things has survived defeat, occupation and urbanization. Much about the Japanese spirit is admirable.

The visitor with only a short time for investigating had best go to Kyoto and such smaller unbombed cities as Kanazawa in search of the outward signs of this spirit: the sudden mossy vision of stillness behind an earthen wall; the fire festival lighting up the summer sky or the temple bell echoing in the winter night; the cleanly appointed, sweet-smelling, rush-matted room that seems to live with the seasons, from the cherry blossoms and the lacy green of early spring, through summer and autumn, to the white dots of flowering plum and the red dots of camellia that keep the Japanese winter from ever being quite dead.

AN observer who has time and patience, however, will presently see that something of all this remains in Tokyo and Osaka, too. They are cities almost without parks, huge growths eating up greenery, but they somehow manage to keep time with the rhythm of the earth, as most great cities have long forgotten how to do. In part this is because they are so largely made up of people just in from the country, but more it is because they are intrinsically Japanese. An ability to respond to nature and become part of its changing lights and moods has long permeated Japanese life and art.

The Sumida River, which flows through Tokyo, is one of the filthiest in the world; but when a person goes boating on a summer night and the breeze brings the plaintive twang of the three-stringed samisen from other boats and perhaps the smell of the fish market (that distilled essence of the country which lives by the sea), he becomes part of the summer itself. The huts along the bank may be miserable; and yet the poor districts of Tokyo, with their reed blinds waving in the summer breeze, their fireflies and crickets bought at some market in delicate bamboo cages, their morning-glories climbing into the night, are not merely sordid, as similar districts of New York or London are. They still have their ties with nature.

So much may be observed by walking the streets and floating on the waters, but it is necessary to go behind walls to find gardens in Japan. This is as true of Kyoto as it is of Tokyo. The quiet lines and colors of Kyoto make it seem like the essence of repose compared to the capital city. For real visions of stillness, however, one has to leave the public streets. A garden nestled against one of the lovely eastern hills of the city does not make use of the hill, but rather—walled, self-contained and involuted—looks in upon itself.

When a garden does attempt to make use of a large, open view, the effect is not the unified one of the great English parks, but somehow fragmented. The observer's interest leaves the broad, over-all view and turns to the self-contained parts. Probably the most famous of the gardens that try to take in a larger view is the Shūgakuin villa northeast of Kyoto. Charming in its details of coves and glens, it is unsatisfying when viewed as a whole.

What has been said of the Shūgakuin can be applied to much Japanese endeavor in the arts. Though often moving in detail, Japanese literary works lack sustained flights. Because of a certain want of body, not much Japanese literature can be described as being of the very first order. In some forms, particularly short poetic ones, the Japanese may be said to lead the world. But when they attempt longer works, these tend, like the garden of the Shūgakuin, to break into their component parts.

JAPANESE prose literature has had two great periods: it flourished in the 10th and 11th Centuries and again in the 17th and 18th. The first, the Heian Period, produced the one true exception to the Japanese tendency toward fragmentation: *The Tale of Genji.* This triumph of fiction is perhaps the world's first great novel. Primarily concerned with the loves of a prince called "the shining Genji," it brims with the life and the feeling for reality that are the essence of any novel, and it has a formal unity, within which its various themes—the Buddhist notion of retribution, the sweet-sad sense of a declining world, the quest for lover-and-parent—are spun out. The author, a court lady named Murasaki, is the supreme literary genius of Japan.

Because of its formal unity and its weaving of themes and characters, *The Genji* is frequently compared to Marcel Proust's *Remembrance of Things Past*. But unlike Proust's work, it is not a highly intellectual book. Japanese writing does not on the whole emphasize the intellect. Essentially *The Genji* is a love story or a series of them, and unity of mood is as important to it as any formal unity. The book is pervaded by a sense of the fleeting beauty of life and the world: "a feeling for things" is perhaps the nearest anyone can come in English to the phrase by which the Japanese characterize the mood. Here is a typical passage from *The Genji*:

"One evening when as usual Genji was pondering on the strange fate that time after time, with so fatal an issue, had bound his fortunes to those of this one family, that intangible thing they call a gossamer-fly flitted across his path. 'I told myself I had caught it, and I thought I held it safe. But when I looked the gossamer-fly had vanished —vanished, or never been in my hand!'

"Such was the poem that he recited sitting alone."

Japanese fiction had its next great day in the 17th Century. Then, however, it specialized in garrulous reporting on the combination of extravagance and frugality that made up urban Japanese life at the time. Charming though it can be, this particular variety of realistic fiction tends to seem frothy, lightweight and fragmentary, and the reader turns rather to poetry in search of the *Genji* legacy.

The typical poem of Murasaki's day was a love poem. In the centuries following her death, poets turned to nature, and the old "feeling for things" deepened into a feeling for what might

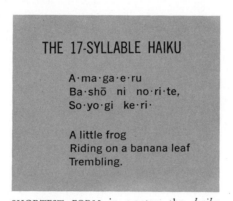

THE 17-SYLLABLE HAIKU

A·ma·ga·e·ru
Ba·shō ni no·ri·te,
So·yo·gi ke·ri·

A little frog
Riding on a banana leaf
Trembling.

SHORTEST FORM in poetry, the *haiku* usually has 17 syllables (*top*). The "o" in *Bashō* (banana plant) counts twice.

be called "the still heart of things." The influence of Zen Buddhism was strong, for Zen has as its goal (not, however, to be expressed in words) a similar insight into the ultimate quietness behind motion, the unity behind diverse phenomena. The poetic form of the 17th Century was the 17-syllable *haiku*, perhaps the shortest in all literature, and Bashō was the master poet:

So still.
And they sink into the rocks,
These voices of locusts.

To the person who has sat in the heavy stillness of the Japanese summer, this is the essence of the matter. The warm air is liquid, and the locusts shrill with an almost tactile intensity.

But *haiku* are essentially untranslatable, and to understand them it is necessary to determine their antecedents. It was in the Middle Ages (roughly 1200 to 1600) that the country's most characteristic esthetic principles were developed. Their emphasis is on understatement—on the simple, even the crude, as a bond with nature and with the stillness behind it.

In those centuries Japanese architecture and Japanese dress developed into something like their present form. Like the Japanese house, the kimono tries to be at one with nature. The morning-glory pattern of mid-summer gives way to the gentian and then to the chrysanthemum and the maple leaf. Here is a modern essayist describing the kimono as it is when the wearer understands it:

"The November day was overcast. A quick autumn shower swept by. The young woman wore an azure kimono dappled with maple leaves, some pale red, some deep red. The three-mat room was dusky even in the daytime, and the kimono seemed to give off its own beautiful light. As she reached to take the lid from the kettle, falling leaves rustled against the roof, and it was as though one or two of them had come inside to make the pattern on her sleeve and shoulder.''

The woman is performing the tea ceremony, a precisely formulated and highly stylized way of making tea with simple but carefully chosen utensils. The ceremony itself was developed in the Middle Ages, and it also was lighted by the Zen vision of the quiet behind the tumultuous. Today it is in danger of being overwhelmed by the profit motive. Significantly, the young heir apparent to the renowned Urasenke, a house whose function it is to watch over one branch of the tea ceremony, was recently elected president of the National Junior Chamber of Commerce—and the nervous bustle of his advertising agents suggested anything but the massive calm of a Zen-inspired master.

As a master would have put it together, the tea ceremony was testimony to a genius for finding truth and beauty in the unadorned. In the soft, changing light of a rustic cottage, the master made tea with utensils that were beautiful yet made no assertion of beauty. The symbolism of the ritual taught the twin Buddhist lessons that life is constant change and that there is Buddhahood in the common clay. If today the ceremony is likely to bring nothing more than a cup of tea and a chance for everyone present to wear a new kimono, in centuries long past it brought repose to warriors who did not know whether they would be alive the next day.

THE principle of understatement also finds expression in the graphic arts of the Middle Ages and in its dramatic form, the Nō play, a dignified, sonorous form that may be compared to the opera in its combination of music and drama, and also to the classical Greek drama.

The kind of medieval painting that was influenced by Zen is restraint itself, only a few strokes of black ink, with perhaps a touch of red or brown. It does not fill the whole of its rectangular space. Rather the white of paper or silk is left to suggest worlds unpainted.

So it is with the Nō, whose slow pace, stylized gestures, masked or impassive faces and strangely hollow noises combine, as the nature images of *haiku* do or the strokes of an ink painting, to take the observer beyond any specific sensual image. The goal of the Nō is a state known as ''mindlessness,'' in which the actor and the action merge and distinctions disappear. A Nō play is like an Italian opera in that it is an amalgam of drama, music and dance, but in spirit the two are quite different. When the Nō play trails off into silence and the players turn and move slowly from the bare stage, it is a silence as if all passion had been over for a long time.

ALL is not restraint in the Japanese spirit, however. There can be an exuberant manner, in which plenty of color is slapped on and nothing is left unsaid—a manner in which, as a matter of fact, most things are said several times.

It may be that the gay, highly colored painting which flourished during the Heian Period is nearer the Japanese heart than the somber ink painting of later centuries. In contrast to the monochromes of medieval Zen, the great Heian picture scrolls sometimes have a sensuous richness of texture and sometimes a sort of slapdash gaiety, and they are known as *Yamato-e* (Japanese paintings). The Japanese are magnificent colorists: a Buddhist scripture can be turned radiantly sensuous by decorations which in effect deny the whole unworldly message. The carefully blended colors of the paper on which a poetess might leave her delicate line of ink can themselves make an abstract painting: a moving, vibrating one against which the calligraphy (an important art in the Orient) speaks with a voice of silence, quiet against motion. Something akin to this genius for color survives in modern Japanese commercial art. The wrapping in which a gift comes is frequently more attractive than the gift.

It is very rare for a Japanese painting to seem gaudy, even when it is highly colored. There is another art, however, to which overstatement is so essential that it may on occasion seem to wander dangerously near the borders of the garish: the drama of the 17th Century and after. It makes use both of puppets and of live actors, and the exaggeration is in part due to the fact that the puppets sometimes overshadow the humans.

JAPANESE puppets are not little Punches and Judys bobbing over whimsical landscapes. They are almost life-size and the manipulators are clearly in view of the audience. In these circumstances, plus the added circumstance that they act not farces but tragedies, the illusion of life is produced by making every gesture twice as big as life. When one first sees a puppet play, the illusion seems impossible to accomplish, the obstacles too great; but presently a strange reversal takes place, and the puppets come to seem like savage little beasts whom the manipulators are trying to restrain.

It was this dramatic style which the live Kabuki actors (in pure Kabuki there are no actresses, only female impersonators) took over. Kabuki was the plebeian drama of the Tokugawa Period, its flash and bluster the reverse of the severe, withdrawn Nō. As in the puppet theater, nothing in Kabuki lacks emphasis, and laughs and sobs alike are among the most racking ever invented by man. The essential fact about Kabuki, however, is that it is a richly visual art. The observer can be repelled by the message of a play, which as likely as not is an exhortation to blind loyalty, whatever cruel and bloody acts this may require; and he may occasionally wish that the character who has disemboweled himself would manage to die a little more quickly and a little less articulately. But he cannot deny the extraordinary beauty of line and color. The art of the dance is essential to Kabuki, and during climaxes in which, in a more realistic dramatic form, there would probably be action, the Kabuki actors are likely to freeze suddenly into a gorgeous tableau, while wooden clappers emphasize the moment and preclude speech.

During the Tokugawa Period, for about two centuries after the rise of the puppet theater, the arts of Japan were shut off from the world. Then, in the middle of the 19th Century, Commodore

Perry arrived and the outside world once more flooded in. Some of the arts—fragile, hothouse products of isolation—were less able to resist than others. Painting had become academic. The polychrome wood-block print that grew out of it had turned with considerable success from people to landscapes, but its great day had been toward the end of the 18th Century. The Nō theater had for centuries simply preserved old forms. In Kabuki, perhaps the liveliest of the arts, the tendency had long been to write display pieces for well-known actors. In literature there was a certain amount of picaresque fun, but most writers either fell into eroticism or continued to report on the townsman's life in a manner that had been done better in the 17th Century. Poetry was at best pretty, at worst stale and trivial. In architecture there had been nothing really new since the Middle Ages.

THE West came pouring in on this somewhat desiccated rock of tradition. Painting was perhaps struck the worst. The masters of the academic style were reduced to penury. One of them painted fans for shipment to China, at the rate of one yen for every hundred fans. Late in the century, with some encouragement from the government and the energetic backing of an American professor named Ernest Fenollosa, a modest renaissance of the traditional styles occurred. But they had little life in them, and although people today continue to produce "Japanese paintings," by which is meant paintings that use traditional materials, the future of Japanese art would seem to lie with an international style that derives ultimately from Paris while making use of a native feeling for line and color. An art exhibit in Tokyo may seem excessively derivative, with a pseudo Matisse here, a pseudo Klee there; but the native spirit does seem to be making itself seen once more beneath the Parisian surfaces. There has been an interesting revival of the wood-block print, again in an international style.

The Nō also had bad days after Perry's arrival, but presently it found its helpers, among them none other than General Ulysses S. Grant.

The general visited Japan in 1879 and advised the Japanese to preserve their Nō drama. The Nō cannot quite be called affluent today, but it does seem secure, supported as it is by carefully organized bodies of people who, in a less austere context, would be called "fans."

Among those who helped the Kabuki was the Emperor Meiji, who attended a performance in 1887 and thus gave the form a respectability it had not previously had. The Kabuki was aided even more by a remarkably talented band of actors whose careers almost spanned the Meiji Period and who were able to move with the times. As a result the Kabuki became a more realistic vehicle than it had previously been.

Yet in spite of the new realism, such Kabuki conventions as the female impersonator made it necessary for those who wanted to go really modern—whether their upbringing was inside or outside the old theatrical tradition—to find themselves a new medium. This they did toward the end of the 19th Century, with original melodramas and adaptations (*The Merchant of Venice* was adapted as *Mercenary Affairs Under the Cherry Blossoms*) that were vaguely realistic in technique. Early in the 20th Century they plunged into the theater of the West, with the Norwegian playwright Henrik Ibsen as their great inspiration. Today Tokyo has an experimental theater whose energy and bravery cannot be denied, even though the productions, for want of time and capital, sometimes have a tacked-together look about them.

TRADITIONAL architecture and allied arts went into eclipse after the Meiji Restoration. The influx of the West left Japan coated with Victorian buildings. Some of them, such as the Iwasaki mansion in Tokyo and the clock tower of Hokkaido University, have now been made "important cultural properties," under the protection of the government. But meanwhile the practicing architects have gone ahead to something new, even while going back to something old. Architects everywhere have begun to notice that the old Japanese house and the modern skyscraper are in principle quite similar: both

are frameworks in which the walls act only as shields or shells and have no structural function. The influence of the Japanese on home architecture throughout the world has been particularly impressive. The Hawaiian Islands and some parts of the American Pacific Coast are beginning to look like Japanese architectural colonies.

ALONG with the modernized drama, the modern novel has been the most sensitive of art forms to influences from the West. At about the turn of the century, Japanese novelists rejected the old written language in favor of the colloquial. Something known as "naturalism" stands at the center of the modern literary scene. It is derived from 19th Century France, and its aim, like that espoused by the French naturalists, is to turn a searching and scientific eye on particular men in particular social situations at particular historical moments. Yet Japanese naturalism ends up as something quite different from the French. It is not about people in social situations, but about people alone. Loneliness is the great theme of the modern Japanese novel.

The modern novel can be uniquely Japanese in other ways, too. Thus Yasunari Kawabata, one of the finest living novelists, considers himself to be under the influence of the French, but in passages like the following the echoes are not French at all:

"From behind the rock, the cedars threw their trunks in perfectly straight lines, so high that he could see the tops only by arching his back. The dark needles blocked out the sky, and the stillness seemed to be singing quietly. The trunk against which Shimamura leaned was the oldest of all. For some reason all the branches on the north side had withered, and, their tips broken and fallen, they looked like stakes driven into the trunk with their sharp ends out, to make a terrible weapon for some god."

The echoes take the reader back to Japanese poetry at the end of the 17th Century. Despite a hundred years of westernization, traces of the Japanese spirit are still very much in evidence.

In quiet contemplation, a Buddhist monk absorbs the silent beauty of the Kohō-An garden at the ancient Daitoku-ji Temple in Kyoto

Stillness Unruffled by the Flow of Time

Outward life in Japan throbs with a fevered pulse, and the cheek-by-jowl congestion of cities appears to dissolve the individual in the crowd. But solace in solitude is still to be found. There can be retreat within the spirit itself or inside the cloistered calm of a garden. The canons of Japanese art, which derive from ancient Buddhism, enjoin the artist to look for and to make order in nature—to find lessons in simple stones, and poems in the lilt of running brooks.

95

SEA OF SAND (*left*), set in a 17th Century garden by landscapist Kobori Enshū outside Kyoto's Nanzenji Temple, swirls around a tree that represents land.

FIGURE OF CLAY, called a *haniwa* (*opposite*), was stationed beside a tomb about 18 centuries ago as a symbol of a servant buried alive with his owner.

EXOTIC PAINTING *is inspired by gods and nature*

FOUR SEASONS (*left*) are dramatically depicted on screens painted for rich 16th Century merchants. Autumn and winter (*top*) are shown in a stormy, moonlit scene, spring and summer (*bottom*) in a green and hilly daytime landscape.

LORD OF LIGHT, the Amida Buddha in a 13th Century screen painting waits with his two attendants to escort faithful souls into paradise. Screens such as this were customarily placed around the deathbeds of the devout to give them consolation.

GUARDIAN of Buddhism, the god Fudo (*left*) was painted in the 12th Century. He holds a rope and a sword for binding and destroying evil powers.

GOD OF WIND on a 17th Century screen painting (*right*) symbolizes Japanese preoccupation with typhoons that ravage the islands from year to year.

SCULPTURE of
wood and metal
through the centuries
shows the varying
moods of awesome gods

PENSIVE SAVIOR, cast in bronze during the Seventh Century (*left*), represents Miroku, Buddhist redeemer of souls.

ANGRY GOD (*opposite*), carved from cypress in the 13th Century, was said to ward off evil spirits from a temple.

HAUGHTY QUEEN (*below*), in wood, was worshiped as a Shinto goddess. The figure was made 10 centuries ago.

FANFARE by a brass band accompanies fireworks at the opener of a baseball series in Osaka. Leading ballplayers now rival *sumō* wrestlers in popularity as sports heroes.

7

Diversions Borrowed and Preserved

THE Japanese are known as great borrowers, but they are also great preservers. And nowhere do they show more talent for importing what is new and exotic, while simultaneously keeping what is old and familiar, than in entertainment and sports. The traditional pleasures and the newly imported ones are able to coexist in peace and prosperity.

Sumō, the oldest form of Japanese wrestling, calls itself "the national sport." Its antiquity gives it a good claim to the title. In the oldest chronicles there is mention of a match in 30 B.C., though the dating is unreliable. Somewhat later an emperor is reported to have diverted himself with lady wrestlers, naked except for the loincloth that is the traditional *sumō* uniform. Japanese literature is full of stories about *sumō*. One legend is that two princes wrestled for the throne of Japan in the Ninth Century. Another has the Ninth Century poet and rake

Narihira wrestling playfully with the emperor's son and falling through the balustrade of the throne dais.

To the expert, *sumō* is a sport of infinite subtlety, each of its holds and throws being as carefully defined and documented as the points of a show dog. The basic rules are nevertheless simple. The contestant may take a grip on the upper part of his opponent's body or on the stiff silk loincloth; he wins a match if he forces his opponent from the ring or makes him touch any part of his body except the soles of his feet to the ground.

To the nonexpert, the most immediately impressive characteristics of *sumō* are the slowness and complexity of the ritual in relation to the brevity of the actual matches, and the extraordinary physical attributes of the wrestlers. Although most Japanese are short in stature, *sumō* wrestlers are huge and weigh three hundred pounds or more. The tallest one in recent memory was more than six and a half feet tall, and the chronicles tell of a 17th Century wrestler who stood at more than eight feet.

THE ritual bespeaks the antiquity of *sumō*. In addition to demonstrating that they have no weapons concealed among their folds of fat, the wrestlers purify themselves with water and purify the ring with salt. Both observances go back to primitive Shinto, with its emphasis on ritual purity, and so to the earliest traditions of the Japanese race. Indeed the ring has a roof, which in olden times would have been supported by pillars but is now suspended from the ceiling of the hall and is supposed to make the ring resemble a shrine.

The preparations also include elaborate feintings, stampings and crouchings, designed to inject a "spiritual" element into the sport. The wrestler who has best succeeded in calming himself and arousing apprehension in the heart of his opponent is held to be in the better position to win when the time allotted for the preparations has finally elapsed.

All of this the spectator watches meditatively from the floor of the hall. There are a few chairs available, but the true devotee spurns them in favor of the rush-matted boxes that surround the ring on all four sides. Seated on a cushion, he keeps beside him a *saké* bottle or a teapot (or both), for the hours are long, the dust can be troublesome, and modest intoxication adds to the pleasant tension as the hour for the principal matches approaches.

AT length the preparations are over and the match begins. The wrestlers spring at each other and a roar rises from the hall. The man who springs first has the advantage, though the real virtuoso will sometimes hold back to demonstrate that he can win anyway. Despite these refinements a match may well be over as soon as it begins (the average time is something like ten seconds), one of the wrestlers having hurtled from the ring; and so the spectator goes back to his tea or *saké* while the next two giants start purifying themselves.

Today this ancient sport is big business. The declared incomes of wrestlers are far lower than those of baseball players in Japan, but fan club arrangements, though elaborate and obscure, are usually profitable for the athletes. On tournament days, almost every radio and television station in the country gives the sport an hour or two of prime evening time.

Yet *sumō* has something quaintly archaic about it. The person who expects to walk briskly up to the box office and buy himself a ticket for a good seat should be advised to save his time and inquire instead at some geisha house. The geisha establishments and a mysterious group of organizations known as "*sumō* teahouses" have ways of assuring, in Tokyo and Osaka at least, that relatively few good seats become available to the public without their intercession.

Relations among wrestlers are not ideally competitive. It is common knowledge that they can be persuaded, under a variety of circumstances, to throw a match, but the situation is so complex that "fix" is probably too strong a word for what happens. For example, a wrestler who has already won enough matches for one of the tournament prizes will sometimes give a match to a hard-pressed comrade who is on the verge of being demoted, on the understanding that the latter will repay the debt once his position is secure again. The public is likely to be less incensed than touched at such evidence of the conspiratorial and non-competitive in what is theoretically a test of strength.

There are six major *sumō* tournaments annually, each lasting fifteen days. The nation therefore focuses its attention on the sport one day out of every four in the year. During the late afternoon hours of the big matches the public baths, normally humming and splashing with after-work crowds, are empty, for everyone is at his television set watching *sumō*. Yet *sumō* has no monopoly on the nation's affections. Alongside it is a new and foreign sport that has become just as national.

INTRODUCED by an American schoolteacher, baseball came to Japan in 1873, three years before the founding of the National League in the U.S. The first international match took place shortly thereafter between a Japanese team and a team of foreigners from Yokohama. No one had informed the Japanese team that it was the catcher's practice to wear a mask. Chagrined at this omission, the Japanese asked for a delay, in the course of which a fencing mask was produced. No such lack of professional deftness would be conceivable today. Japanese players are highly skilled, and in 1960 the Tokyo Giants defeated the visiting San Francisco Giants. Japanese newspapers have reported that the American major leagues have tried to get the third baseman of the Tokyo team.

It would be hard to say which of the two sports, *sumō* or baseball, is the more popular. Television brings both to the whole nation. But baseball plays to bigger crowds. Attendance at ball parks is enormous, running to eight or nine million a year for the two professional leagues. In 1959 the Tokyo Giants attracted an average of more than 20,000 people per game, and when their opponents were the Osaka Tigers the figure pushed 30,000. The income of baseball players is as obscure as that of *sumō* wrestlers, but the talk among observers of the sport is that the biggest star of a recent season allowed a bonus of ¥30 million (the equivalent of about $83,000) to lure him onto the team owned by the National Railways.

Japanese baseball has taken on certain marks of its own. Cheering sections at amateur and semiprofessional games are vociferous. But the crowds at professional games tend to be quieter than in the United States, and to applaud gently, as if they were at a tennis match. The player who fails to run out a close play is seldom subjected to the derision he could expect in any American ball park. Until very recently it was the custom (almost never honored in the U.S.) for fly balls to be returned from the stands.

The Japanese world series is more elaborately staged than its American counterpart: pretty girls lead the parades of players, there are lavish fireworks displays, and brass bands delight the audience with tunes like "Frankie and Johnny." Yet the game remains the American game, and the standard of excellence in play is American. Baseball is therefore a bond with the United States.

In some imported sports, notably such individual ones as boxing, swimming and gymnastics, the Japanese produce world champions. In certain team sports—baseball is one—they are very competent, but not quite the best in the world. In others they do what they can, though their physique is against them. Not many Japanese are beefy enough for American football or tall enough for basketball, and yet they are always playing "bowl games" with American service football teams, and they religiously send a basketball team to the Olympics to lose in an early round.

AMONG the more esoteric of the traditional sports is one from the Heian Period called *kemari*. Even today bands of people gather from time to time to kick around deerskin balls in the Heian style just as the hero of *The Tale of Genji* did a thousand years ago. This interesting pastime is in a way the reverse of soccer, for its immediate purpose is not to keep the ball away from the opponent but rather to kick it to a companion (there are no opponents) so that he too can have his kick, and the ball moves around swiftly.

Other sports hover on the border between the traditional and the new. *Karate*, which literally means "empty hands," is a lethal sort of fist and foot fighting that has been stylized almost into a dance. It developed in Okinawa several centuries ago, and became popular in Japan at about the time of World War I. More abstruse is duck netting, which was invented in the Meiji Period and which has all the sedate, non-competitive qualities of Heian soccer. Not everyone is privileged to indulge in this sport, for the enthusiast must wangle an invitation to one of the imperial duck preserves. Once inside, he advances upon a ditch in a line with other participants. He clutches a very large net, and he hopes that one of the ducks in the ditch, startled by the appearance of the intruders, will fly into the net. More often than not, one of them does, such being the size of the nets and the small margin for escape allowed the ducks. For the person so uncertain of hand and eye that he can never hope to bag a duck with a gun, the sport is a fine one—except on warm days, when the ducks are sometimes too sleepy to start up into the nets.

A S the statistics on baseball attendance suggest, the Japanese, like most urbanized peoples, are becoming a nation of spectators. Sand-lot baseball is everywhere, to be sure; but inside the home, television, radios and phonographs provide the standard entertainment. The notion of family fun around the hearth has never been a very important part of Japanese life. The one exception comes at the New Year, when tradition requires a family to indulge in such pursuits as the matching of the "One Hundred Poems" cards. In this genteel pastime the person chosen as umpire reads the first half of a well-known poem, and the competitors vie to be first in finding, from the cards spread out before them, the card that carries the second half of the poem. A real expert can generally find the

second half after no more than two or three syllables have been read from the first.

For the rest of the year, the members of the family tend to go their various ways. When the children are very young, their parents will take them occasionally to the zoo. When they are somewhat older and ready to engage in the frantic national pastime of travel, they usually do it with their school comrades rather than their parents. Especially in the spring and fall, every moderately well-known spot in the country is so overrun with students as to make the unaccompanied tourist feel quite overwhelmed. Japanese of all ages shun solitary travel, preferring to move about in large groups. The National Railways are beginning to lose considerable revenue to chartered buses.

F OR the younger members of the family, moving pictures are the favorite entertainment. Although a patriotic film now and then makes a great hit with the middle-aged and thereby temporarily forces up the average age of the movie audience, the typical moviegoer is in his early 20s. He has much to choose from. The Japanese turn out more movies than any other nation in the world—more than 500 feature-length films per year as against some 200 for the United States. In spite of the hold which *sumō* and baseball broadcasts have on the nation, the average Japanese sees at least one movie a month. This is about the same per capita consumption as in the United States, and in 1959 there were more movie theaters in Japan in proportion to the population than there were in the United States. The number of theaters is also growing, whereas in the United States it is falling off slightly.

High-quality movies are exported and well received abroad, where their stylization and pictorial beauty are much admired—and justly so. Yet the Japanese have not escaped the lures of tawdry mass culture. A Japanese critic recently remarked that only one Japanese film in 20 would dare show its face outside Japan. Typical fare for home consumption are the sentimental melodrama and the samurai picture. The former often portrays bereaved and otherwise troubled mothers, so much so that there is a special type known as "the mother piece." The samurai film, which is akin to the American western, has conventions like those of its U.S. counterpart. Just as the cowboy is alone among men in being able to shoot a pistol accurately from a galloping horse, so the samurai is always able to find victims who are obliging enough to fall upon his sword. The most famous of all exported Japanese movies, *Rashōmon*, a psychological study in a medieval setting, owes some of its bluster to this tradition.

It may be of significance that the typical family situation in recent Japanese movies is that of the American comic strip *Blondie:* the wife is strong, the husband weak. One cannot be sure whether the American comic strip or the modern Japanese family is the model, but in any event Japanese audiences seem prepared to accept a reversal of traditional arrangements (domineering husband, submissive wife) in the films they see. Movie daughters tend to be strong too, and quite without principles.

IF the movies are chiefly for the younger members of the family, the older members also have their pleasures. Among the more interesting and traditional are those that are likely today to go with the father's expense account —especially the geisha party.

The word "geisha" literally means "accomplished person," and the original function of the geisha was to sing and dance at parties. The charm of the geisha party is not always immediately apparent, however, since the accomplished persons are likely to be somewhat jerky little creatures whose games, rather like "Simon says thumbs up," wholly impede conversation, and whom it is the guest's duty to entertain—not the reverse. Yet something does manage to get accomplished, it would seem, for a large proportion of the business affairs of Japan are transacted in geisha houses, and geisha have on occasion become important personages. A Kyoto geisha is said to have been one of the powers behind Takayoshi Kido, who was one of the prime

movers of the Meiji Restoration. Such arrangements are an afterglow of Tokugawa Japan, when much of the townsmen's culture centered upon such pleasure quarters as the Yoshiwara in Edo (today's Tokyo), the Shimabara in Kyoto, the Shimmachi in Osaka and the Maruyama in Nagasaki. In a society that tried to strangle him with rules of Confucian propriety and in any case branded him the most contemptible of its members, the merchant at least had his pleasure quarter to flee to.

YET though the geisha in her original form was a skilled entertainer, it is not possible to dispose completely of the notion that she is a prostitute. There are all sorts of geisha, and geisha and prostitute merge into each other by imperceptible stages. When the hero of a modern novel by Yasunari Kawabata asks for a geisha, it is quite clear that he does not want singing and dancing, and in the novels of Kafū Nagai, the great authority on such matters, ladies whose only accomplishments are those of the bedchamber happily call themselves geisha. At the other extreme are aloof and frequently elderly ladies who are among the better musicians and dancers of the land.

It is in large measure because of the truly accomplished geisha that a richness of traditional art and entertainment does survive in Japan. As Kafū Nagai said in 1909: "Under the law today, theirs is held to be an improper and unseemly profession; but it is they who make the donations by which the beauty of shrines and temples remains to decorate the city, and it is they who encourage the Japanese drama with gifts of curtains and the like. If, in this day of Europeanizing, we did not have the world of the pleasure quarters, the music and the drama of Edo would have quite disappeared. We must be eternally grateful."

In the traditional theater arts (which in Japan include both music and the dance, for they are closely allied to the stage), almost no styles or forms are allowed to die. Each artistic faction or school is organized as if it were a family, with an *iemoto,* or "head of the house," presiding.

It is the *iemoto* who guards the purity of the school's artistic forms, and it is he who licenses its teachers—often for a sizeable fee. Even when there is very little for the *iemoto* to preside over, the right of succession to the post is carefully preserved.

Sometimes music and dance forms do come upon bad days. The *iemoto* may be a wastrel who absconds in the night, or the art may be so utterly unpromising that no one cares to be honored with the title *iemoto*. The one-stringed lyre, popular in the late Edo (or Tokugawa) and early Meiji Periods, but on the verge of disappearing today, is an example of a form of music that is no longer capable of attracting an *iemoto*. More often the problem is the opposite: the *iemoto* of a thriving school dies, and all sorts of people would like to succeed him. A fierce squabble thereupon breaks out over the succession, and the school splits into several parts, each new faction headed by an important disciple of the late *iemoto*.

The more prosperous the school, the greater the possibility of such a split. Because the ability to perform something resembling a traditional dance is still a mark of a well-reared maiden in Japan, the major dance schools continue to be very prosperous. In a single 12-month period in 1957 and 1958, there were splits in almost all of them. One school managed to avoid such an upheaval by a complicated and uniquely Japanese compromise. Its *iemoto* gave up his title and assumed another name. His mother-in-law thereupon took custody of the title, on the understanding that she would pass it on to her daughter (the wife of the former *iemoto*) when the latter's art "ripened."

IN the entertainment world and in the dramatic arts, as in sports, the traditional forms are not the only popular ones. The Japanese are willing to try almost everything, and the new and the old live side by side.

It is on record that the Japanese Christians of the 16th Century took to playing western harps and flutes, and a slight echo of western music persisted in Japan all through the centuries of seclusion. The little horns with which noodle vendors still attract customers on winter nights carry a Portuguese name. In 1894 a group of foreigners and Japanese performed the first act of Gounod's opera *Faust* in Tokyo; less than a decade later the Japanese were ready to try opera on their own, doing so with a production of Gluck's *Orpheus*.

AGAIN as in sports, the Japanese are very brave about engaging in activities in which nature would seem to be against them. Dressed in tights and asked to perform a ballet, the stocky Japanese physique somehow never quite seems to get off the ground. Yet the Japanese have for years been determined ballet dancers. In 1912 an Italian ballet master was summoned to Japan, and three years later the Japanese had an independent troupe. Today the Japanese ballet still thrives, although one critic remarked recently after looking back over a year's performances that the local dance was "somewhat overwhelmed" by western ballet.

In recent years foreign ballerinas have made it a practice to bring their regular partners with them when going on tours of Japan. In the old days, however, the visiting stars would come alone and rely on native talent to support them, and when the long-limbed dancer from abroad flung herself upon her small Japanese partner, a gasp of apprehension, and then a titter, would sweep the hall.

Ballroom dancing and jazz also flourish, and Japanese singers with exotic foreign names are conspicuous among suppliers of popular music. Peggy Hayama, Frank Nagai, and a pair of twins known (in English) as "The Peanuts" scored smash hits in 1959. The names do not fool very many people, however. The nasal delivery of Peggy and Frank could only be Japanese, and somewhere in their bright, up-to-date, Americanized strains, one catches a plaintive note of pre-modern Japan.

They and many other performers have made Tokyo the night club capital of the Orient, perhaps of the world, even while it remains a museum of old cultural forms.

Window-gazers view a scale model of Tokyo before seeing the actual panorama of the city from high up in the 1,092-foot Tokyo Tower

A Zeal for Overcrowded Amusements

The Japanese are known as the hardest-working folk on earth. They also play as hard as they work. If gentle, solitary pleasures like flower arranging and composing *haiku* poems still attract many devotees, most Japanese prefer more strenuous and gregarious amusements. Families love to tire themselves out on summer outings. Millions of skiers flock to the mountains in winter. And all year long, vast audiences happily endure the crowded ordeal of spectator sports.

JUDO PLAYERS, wearing traditional white trousers and jackets with colored belts (*left*), limber up in a Tokyo gymnasium before engaging in bouts.

SUMO GIANT, weighing 300 pounds (*opposite*), crouches on the sand of the ring with his hands clenched, watching for a chance to attack his foe.

GEISHA GIRLS *give style to social life. They are not only elegant companions but skilled entertainers. Witty conversation, now a rarity in their profession, is more prized than beauty*

ON PARADE during Kyoto's annual geisha festival, this woman (*left*) wears a costume traditional to her calling for 300 years. Her face is lacquered with cosmetics.

ON STAGE in Kyoto's Minamiza Theater, kneeling geisha from the world-famous Gion quarter of the ancient Japanese capital welcome the spring with the gay *Miyako Odori*, called a "cherry dance" by westerners, which is performed from April 1 till May 10. The dancers move gracefully to the music of strings, flutes, drums and bells.

KABUKI, *a form of musical drama, is closely related to puppetry*

LION DANCER, playing a classic Kabuki role, wears rich robes and a luxuriant mane (*opposite*). His *kumadori*, or make-up, is intended to make his face masklike.

WARRIOR PUPPET three quarters life size is manipulated by two men in the *Bunraku* drama. One of them (*right*) wears black to give an illusion of invisibility.

Zen monks of the Rinzai sect, seeking "salvation through meditation and a divine emptiness," sit cross-legged in contemplation in a hall

The Tolerant Believers

of the Myōshinji Temple in Kyoto. Buddhism claims about 45 million followers in Japan, of whom one fifth are Zen adherents

JAPAN cannot be characterized as a country of any single religion, as Pakistan is a Moslem country or Spain a Catholic one. On the contrary, Japan is a country of several religions, and for the most part they rest upon it lightly.

Statistics on "believers" are impressive, the number of faithful adding up to considerably more than the total population of the country. Indeed, if Japanese below the age of consent are removed from consideration, it would seem that virtually everyone is counted as a twofold believer. What this means is that most Japanese are sufficiently tolerant of Shinto and Buddhism to participate in the rituals of both. Traditionally, a third great force, Confucianism, has lived peacefully beside these two. It shows itself today less in rituals than in lingering notions of duty —notions considered feudal and old-fashioned by the young.

Shinto is the first religion to come into the life of the young Japanese. Particularly if he is born in a rural area, he is likely to be presented at a local shrine shortly after birth, and so introduced to the god under whose jurisdiction he

119

will live. There may also be ceremonies (of very great antiquity) to keep the young spirit from wandering. No doubt because of high infant mortality, the relationship between body and spirit in the early years has been considered tenuous and fickle. At some time early in life the crisis is believed past, and the youngster is taken once more to a shrine, this time to be introduced as a full-fledged person whose spirit is firmly in tow.

A relic of this practice may be found even in the large cities: the Seven-Five-Three rites of November 15. Boys aged five and three and girls aged seven and three are dressed in their best and—uniformly armed with bags of "thousand-year candy," which insures long life—presented at some shrine. A novelist has recently provided information suggesting that whatever religious significance may remain is strongest among the poor. She observed that on November 15 of one year the size of the offering to the shrine varied in inverse proportion to the richness of the child's dress.

Shinto also has a virtual monopoly on weddings. An advanced, modern young couple will sometimes note that because civil procedures are in any case necessary besides whatever religious ceremonies are observed, the latter might as well be dispensed with. Christians may also be suspicious of shrines and priests. But almost everyone else goes through Shinto rituals, complete with go-betweens, even though an increasing number of urban couples come together by their own design rather than by those of marriage arrangers.

On auspicious days in the spring and fall (people tend not to be married in the inclement seasons), crowds of affianced persons, go-betweens and relatives pour in and out of the large shrines, grist for the efficient wedding mill. Though the organdy veil and the bridal train are becoming somewhat more common, most brides still prefer the kimono and high, cloth-capped coiffure of tradition. Bridegrooms are almost always in morning coats and striped trousers. Whatever the garb, the swishing of

sacred branches and the drinking of *saké* are pure Shinto. The proceedings are speeded up a little, perhaps, to fit the busy schedule of the shrine, but they are fundamentally unchanged from very ancient times. Few Japanese feel really married unless they have taken the prescribed nine sips of *saké*.

But not all rituals and beliefs are Shinto. Faith in fortune tellers is widespread, and their origins go back into Chinese prehistory. Even a member of the intelligentsia will sometimes consult a master of divination in selecting a name for a child, or, indeed, a substitute one for himself, if he feels that the products of his artistic or commercial talents should be tagged with a more elegant and fetching name than the one his parents gave him.

Even in the heart of Tokyo, a person who has just bought a house can be a victim of augury. If he is to take possession on February 1, say, he must consider it sufficient cause for having the contract violated if the current occupant has consulted an almanac and discovered that it would be dangerous to move until such time as the winter solstice is further away than the vernal equinox.

THE ceremonies associated with death and the dead are largely Buddhist. Funerals, memorial services and cemeteries provide the chief income of Buddhist temples, except for the famous few that live off tourists. In a recent short story, one of the characters, a young student priest, describes the limited nature of the profession for which he is preparing himself:

"I knew when people would come calling us. In a certain house a certain person dies. A person of this world disappears from this world. Those who are left come to think that we are necessary. They remember that in this world there is a group of aliens who have connections with the other world. They come for us. We take our places like experts beside the corpse."

The idea of life after death is prominent in Japanese folklore and festivals, though not always clearly or systematically formulated. Information about apparitions is detailed: they have no feet, they come at two in the morning "when the grasses sleep," they are likely to be encountered beneath willows by river banks on rainy nights, and they do a great deal of complaining.

The dead are the focus of the greatest festival in Japan, the midsummer Bon. Everyone who possibly can goes home to the country for it. In the cities Bon has been set at mid-July under the Gregorian calendar, but in the countryside it still reaches its climax under a July or August full moon—whichever of the two months contains the seventh full moon under the old Chinese lunar calendar. At the beginning of the festival, lanterns or torches escort the spirits of the dead from cemeteries to the houses that once were theirs. During the several days of the festival the spirits, together with everyone else, are feasted, invited to dance and otherwise made to feel at home. Then, under the full moon, they are escorted back to their resting place again, sometimes with bonfires, sometimes with the lanterns that escorted them at the beginning of the festival, sometimes aboard lighted boats drifted out to sea or down a river.

Japan offers no more moving and beautiful sight than a little provincial coastal village on the last night of Bon. Pale green jewels of lanterns trail up the hills to the cemeteries, which are like swarms of fireflies in a mist—the smoke from the incense seeing the dead back to the skies. Down at the waterfront those whose dead are buried far away see them off on tiny, candlelit boats, white jewels on the receding tide. The silver light suffusing the scene makes one realize how much has been lost in the cities, where the full moon is no longer a part of the festival.

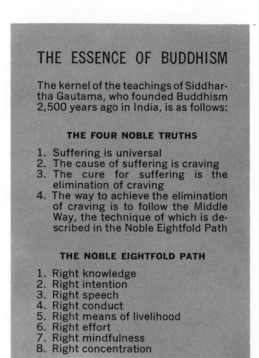

THE ESSENCE OF BUDDHISM

The kernel of the teachings of Siddhartha Gautama, who founded Buddhism 2,500 years ago in India, is as follows:

THE FOUR NOBLE TRUTHS

1. Suffering is universal
2. The cause of suffering is craving
3. The cure for suffering is the elimination of craving
4. The way to achieve the elimination of craving is to follow the Middle Way, the technique of which is described in the Noble Eightfold Path

THE NOBLE EIGHTFOLD PATH

1. Right knowledge
2. Right intention
3. Right speech
4. Right conduct
5. Right means of livelihood
6. Right effort
7. Right mindfulness
8. Right concentration

Of the major religions, Shinto—literally "the way of the gods"—has been in the country the longest. It is the native Japanese faith. In its fundamentals Shinto is not an organized body of thought. It is rather the worship of myriads of natural deities, with great emphasis laid on ritual cleanliness. The Japanese feeling for nature and fondness for washing would thus seem to be very ancient.

Primitive Shinto offered only vague explanations of spirit and the afterworld. It was no match for the subtleties and precise formulations of Buddhism, which began in India and came to Japan in the Sixth Century from China and Korea.

Buddhism in its essentials is aimed at enlightenment through liberation from passion and illusion. Since a fundamental illusion is held to be that of individual being, Buddhism ultimately points toward the extinction of individuality.

Yet Buddhism in China and Japan has taken so many different forms that it sometimes seems to cancel itself out. Some sects believe everyone can become a Buddha or "blessed one," free from illusion and liberated from the cycle of birth and death, while others are more cautious in dangling that prospect. Zen, an austere teaching, insists upon self-cultivation and discipline: liberation is possible only through trials and efforts, and only for a few. The popular pietist sects, on the other hand, urge pure faith and an abandonment to the saving grace of some favored Buddha. He who gives himself to the lord Amida will spend an eternity in the Western Paradise, even though he may have been notably unsuccessful at conquering individual passion. Yet all of these various sorts

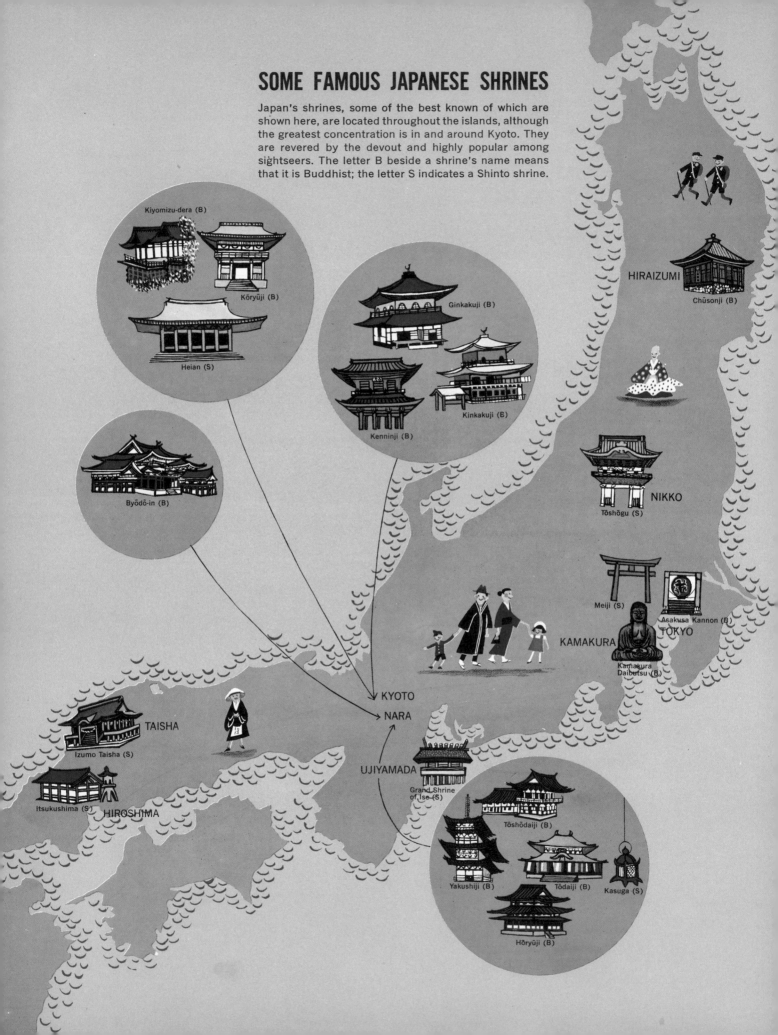

SOME FAMOUS JAPANESE SHRINES

Japan's shrines, some of the best known of which are shown here, are located throughout the islands, although the greatest concentration is in and around Kyoto. They are revered by the devout and highly popular among sightseers. The letter B beside a shrine's name means that it is Buddhist; the letter S indicates a Shinto shrine.

Kiyomizu-dera (B)

Kōryūji (B)

Heian (S)

Ginkakuji (B)

Kinkakuji (B)

Kenninji (B)

Byōdō-in (B)

HIRAIZUMI

Chūsonji (B)

NIKKO

Tōshōgu (S)

Meiji (S)

Asakusa Kannon (B)

KAMAKURA

TOKYO

Kamakura Daibutsu (B)

KYOTO

NARA

TAISHA

Izumo Taisha (S)

UJIYAMADA

Grand Shrine of Ise (S)

Itsukushima (S)

HIROSHIMA

Tōshōdaiji (B)

Yakushiji (B)

Tōdaiji (B)

Kasuga (S)

Hōryūji (B)

of Buddhism are alike in emphasizing the evanescence and insubstantiality of material things.

In the earliest centuries after its introduction into the country, Buddhism was the religion of the aristocracy. Shinto was the folk religion—though it was not wholly discarded by the aristocracy. During the Middle Ages (roughly 1200 to 1600) the pietist sects succeeded in disseminating a popular form of Buddhism. But there was no fundamental conflict with Shinto, for, as early as the Eighth Century, Buddhism had reached an accommodation with the "eight million gods" of Shinto. They were thenceforth seen as manifestations of the ultimate Buddha, and so did not have to be discarded by anyone being converted to one of the new Buddhist sects. Thus was established in its essential features the union of the two that persists today. The person who marries by Shinto rites is generally buried by Buddhist rites.

In the Muromachi Period (the 14th to 16th Centuries) Shinto came to acquire an organized theology of its own, a development that was to affect its place in modern Japan. As the imperial court came upon the hardest times in its history, the cult of the imperial ancestors, and notably of the greatest of the Shinto eight million deities, the Sun Goddess, became the rallying creed for the court's supporters. It was this creed, strengthened and elaborated during and after the 18th Century, that was used to build the State Shinto of modern times—the cult of the mystic family-state headed by the emperor. Today Shinto has been divested of its ultranationalism and would seem to be fairly well back where it began, as the loosely organized worship of myriads of natural deities.

A third way of thought, Confucianism, entered Japan at about the same time as Buddhism and is commonly ranged beside Buddhism and Shinto as one of the traditional Japanese religions. Whether it should be called a religion at all, however, is doubtful. In China it was a philosophy elevating the Chinese state and tributary states to the level of a universal system. In Japan it became an ethical code that glorified scholarship and paid careful attention to notions of duty. As the official code of the Tokugawa shogunate, it had little to say about other worlds, but made a number of emphatic points about this one, most notably about the obligations of inferior to superior.

As the Japanese accepted Shinto, Buddhism and Confucianism, so they would perhaps have tolerated and even accepted Christianity if it had come at a more propitious time. The possibility that one idea may conflict with another has not usually worried the Japanese. Thus they can be simultaneously Confucians and Buddhists—even though this requires a simultaneous belief in existence and nonexistence.

A more important reason for the Japanese tolerance of disparate faiths might have been that a growing indifference to religion itself began to overtake the Japanese at some time toward the end of the Middle Ages. Coincidentally, this process started at about the time that secularization was beginning in the West. There are many parallels between Japanese history and that of western Europe, but surely one of the most striking is that in both places, along with the development of a merchant economy, the minds of men began to turn from another world to this one.

THE beginning of the process may be placed somewhere in the Muromachi shogunate, or in the 14th and 15th Centuries. It was at that time that the pietist sects of Buddhism were beginning to concern themselves with practical matters. Their great leaders during these centuries were not theologians so much as organizers and teachers of secular ethics. Their message of salvation through faith made it possible to leave the work of other worlds to the object of that faith, and to turn to this world instead as the only one in which a man's works made any difference.

By the time of the Tokugawa Period, Confucian teachers were preaching the nobility of commercial affairs, and in their glorification of the merchant they were not very far from the philosophy of Benjamin Franklin: "God gives all things to industry" and "The second vice is lying, the first is running in debt." From this association of mercantile virtues with religion, it is not very difficult to go a step further and put the conception of a deity entirely out of one's mind. The deity is still off there somewhere, but the marketplace need not stand in fear of his wrath.

THE process of secularization was fairly well accomplished by the end of the 18th Century. A most important fact in Japanese religious history is therefore the growing indifference to religion. Yet, as ritual observance at key points in Japanese life suggests, it would be wrong to say that Japan is wholly without religion. One might say, perhaps, that gods do not weigh heavily on Japanese minds. If India may be taken as an example of a country inundated by religion, Japan is near the other extreme, a dry sort of country where there is a shower of faith from time to time that drains smoothly away. Religion does not offer much competition to such persuasive secular philosophies as Marxism.

It does offer certain pleasures, however. The Japanese are great lovers of festivals, most of them Shinto in origin. The midsummer Bon is now considered Buddhist, but its origins are probably Shinto. Much as Christianity in its earliest days took over some very primitive festival marking the end of the dark part of the year and called it Christmas, Buddhism probably accommodated itself to the ancient folk practices of Shinto.

But most festivals do not even pretend to be Buddhist. They are Shinto in name as well as pedigree. On a festival day the sobriety of ordinary days departs. The characteristic feature of the Shinto festival is the portable shrine in which the god receives a very bouncy ride around his domain. Even in crowded sections of Tokyo, traffic stops while the shrine bearers weave their noisy, garrulous way down the street, with frequent pauses for *saké*. On the warm May days of the great Asakusa festival, the observer feels in the air what the statistics

have already revealed, that Tokyo is a city of the young. The old may complain that the god received a more jolting ride when they were young, but it is hard to imagine a more energetic bouncing than he gets today.

The fundamental teachings of the traditional religions have become buried in all the miscellaneous observances, which do little to help people who may wonder what the world is about. The vogue for Marxism is perhaps one consequence; another is the rash of new religious sects. The Japanese have long had a way of turning in times of crisis to new religious leaders. Late in the Tokugawa Period a farm woman named Miki Nakayama founded a faith-healing sect that is today a great power in the land. More recently, a female religious leader announced to the nation that the divinity taken from the emperor by General MacArthur had been transferred to her (whether or not it was bestowed by General MacArthur was not clear). In 1958 the Ministry of Education listed 156 new religions. Total membership in the new sects was estimated at five million—70 per cent female, 80 per cent urban and 90 per cent middle-aged and above.

SOME of the sects are very disreputable. Others are powers to be reckoned with. The Sōkagakkai, which urges its members to be unstinting in their work, has given the labor movement genuine concern in certain coal-mining districts. It elected six candidates to the upper house of the Diet in 1959.

The new religions have something in common with Marxism. Although their leaders may claim divinity, the remedies they offer are of this world and not the next. A typical one promises immediate release from "poverty, illness and strife," the last term apparently referring to family problems. If the new religions tend to be spurned by the young and by men, they are nevertheless evidence of a need to believe. A highly secularized people and a people with whom religion does not appear to count for very much, the Japanese are still susceptible to the pull of dogma.

Pilgrims buy amulets, hot snacks and cold drinks at kiosks in the court of the Myōhōji Temple in Tokyo during the Oeshiki festival

Faith That Does Not Trouble the Soul

The Japanese people are not haunted by the past, but manage to live with it and enjoy it at the same time. They celebrate feasts in honor of their medieval saints with the gusto of Europeans at festivals in the Middle Ages, but the temple-goers now carry transistor radios and cameras. Ancient superstitions and modern electronic miracles are equally taken for granted. But while religion leaves the Japanese unruffled, it has made a deep imprint on their folkways.

GIANT FISH, fashioned of bamboo covered with painted cloth (*opposite*), is launched each July by Toyahama fishermen in honor of the ocean gods.

ROADSIDE SHRINE near Karatsu (*right*) is one of thousands of Shinto holy places at which devout passersby pause to offer their prayers each day.

VISITING THE BEREAVED, Fujiwara conducts a prayer to comfort members of a family that has lost a mother.

INSPECTING SCROLLS (*left*) in his temple sacristy, Fujiwara leaves his shoes outside the door, as piety demands.

BEARING GIFTS of rice (*opposite*) for the dead, the old women of Fujiwara's parish make the rounds of graveyards.

A BUDDHIST PRIEST, *Zosho Fujiwara, offers guidance and consolation to the people of the island of Naoshima off the northern coast*

SEETHING MASS of yelling youths, naked except for loincloths, struggle for possession of two sacred rods cast among them by a priest. This ancient rite in honor of the Buddhist deity Kannon is held each January in the temple at Saidaiji. Possession of either rod, it is said, brings a lifetime of happiness.

Uniformed pupils at a girls' high school in suburban Tokyo pack the verandas of a revolutionary new building. The curving windows

fill the wedge-shaped classrooms with abundant light for study

9

Powerful Molders of Young Minds

THE Japanese people are almost universally equipped with the tools for acquiring knowledge, and they have great riches of printed matter to choose from. Their literacy rate, 98 per cent, is the second highest in the world (only Sweden's is higher). They are among the world's greatest readers, or at least buyers, of newspapers. The number of titles that the Japanese publishing industry turns out every year is among the highest per capita in the world. If it is true that people need only be given the ability to read and plenty of books and newspapers, and the race will automatically move ahead, Japan would seem to be in a happy position. Yet a question remains: In what direction are these vast resources for shaping minds actually doing their work?

The prewar educational system was in many respects a good one: the literacy rate even in the 1930s was approximately what it is today. The system was more European than American. Elementary education was provided for everyone, but the graduates of primary schools were divided into three groups: those who went to work immediately, those who went on for a few years of lower secondary school or specialized vocational training, and the elite few who aimed at the senior high schools and thereby almost automatically went to the universities. The system relied heavily on memory work and did little to encourage imaginative speculation.

Competition for the high schools was intense. The notion that everyone had a right to a college education was, as in England and Germany, quite foreign to the system. But the system was justly administered. Although the son of the tenant farmer was at a great disadvantage in not being able to take time out for advanced study, there was nothing to bar him from the great, virtually tuition-free national universities if he was bright enough to get into one of the public senior high schools.

The notion of educating an elite was repellent to the leaders of the American Occupation, who set about increasing the number of universities by elevating most of the old senior high schools. The theory was that with an enormous number of universities to choose from, students would find each institution much like the next, and the competition to enter the old universities would decrease. The nation would thereby become filled with well-rounded college graduates, one not much different from another.

THESE hopes were soon defeated, for the Occupation authorities did not reckon with the nature of Japanese society. Because belonging to the right clique or faction is deemed so important to personal success and status, ambitious Japanese try to join an influential group at a young age, and this in turn means that it is important to go to the right university. In effect the reform simply intensified and prolonged the competition for admission to the best schools and universities.

Under the old system, students who were admitted to the senior high schools had relatively little trouble moving along into the universities. Now the myriad high schools of the land

pour their graduates out upon the narrow gates of the traditionally honored national universities. Competition for entrance into Tokyo University and Kyoto University, the two top institutions, is so fierce that the chances of being admitted to either of them on the first try are small and diminishing, and an ambitious student is likely to take the entrance examinations year after year rather than settle for a lesser university. Each year aging and weary freshmen enter Tokyo University after having waited five or six years for the honor.

The reason for the pull of Tokyo and Kyoto Universities is simple. Graduates of the two universities have an inside track on successful careers in big business, finance and government. Since shortly after the surrender of 1945, every prime minister, with just one exception, has been a graduate of one university or the other.

IN terms of years spent in various types of schools, the reformed Japanese system is exactly like the American one in those parts of the United States where the junior high school is standard. In other words, a student goes to elementary school for six years, to "lower secondary" for three and "upper secondary" for three. But for complicated reasons, the change to this system meant the introduction of a new system of high schools just below the universities. Again for a complexity of reasons, the new high schools are not up to the standard of the old ones, which were elite establishments. The result is that in spite of intense competition to get past the entrance examinations, the university freshman today is about at the level of the freshman in the prewar senior high school.

The fact that the university graduate is not as well educated as he used to be is much lamented. In the days when the prewar system and the postwar one overlapped, employers had a marked preference for graduates of the old system. The education reform also had the effect of cutting short the only boisterous time a young student had to look forward to: his high school days, when almost everything was permitted him, and his shabby student uniform

—the shabbier the better—set young hearts to fluttering. Students in the new high schools do not have the old verve.

The Occupation could not have foreseen all these developments, but it must be held accountable for one rather serious difficulty. This has to do not with the structure of the educational system but with its content and methods.

ONLY a few months after the start of its rule, the Occupation decided—on the recommendation of a group of American educators who formed a U.S. Education Mission—that rote memory had played too big a part in Japanese education. It was therefore decreed that strong doses of the pragmatic methods recommended by the late American philosopher John Dewey should be administered. According to this theory, the acquisition of knowledge should be a response to the challenges of the world, not an accumulation of so much inert mental baggage. Here, in a summary of the educators' report, is the pertinent message:

"In order that the newer aims of education may be achieved, teaching methods emphasizing memorization, conformity and a vertical system of duties and loyalties should be modified to encourage independent thinking, the development of personality, and the rights and responsibilities of democratic citizenship. The teaching of morals, for example, should be less by precept than by instruction deriving from experiences in concrete situations in school and community."

A subject known as *shakaika*, or "social studies," thereupon became a crucial part of the primary and lower secondary school curriculum —that is, of the nine years of compulsory education. In "social studies" children learn from experience. They are supposed to look upon the society around them and so to discern the principles governing it, and themselves in it.

To an American or an Englishman, there may seem to be nothing at all wrong either with the recommendations of the U.S. mission or with "social studies." The trouble, however, is that the average primary school student in Japan, if not elsewhere, is much too immature to develop principles of his own. Rather he is at the mercy of his teacher's principles, and anything as vaguely defined as "social studies" gives the teacher free rein.

One favorite teaching device used in "social studies" is the excursion: a class of primary students may be taken out on a tour of the other side of town so that they may understand the inequalities of wealth. Another device is the introspective composition: youngsters may be asked to set down their thoughts in "self-reflection" on the quiet desperation of their parents' lives and on possible remedies.

If the teachers happen to be—as John Dewey was—firm believers in a free, pluralistic society, and strong skeptics about the absolute validity of any single explanation of society and history, then in the course of several years the pupil may develop a similar independence of mind. But what if a teacher does not measure up to this high standard? What if he yearns for a "classless" society, a proletarian dictatorship free of the clutter and inefficiency of democracy? The trouble with "learning from experience" is that it provides no defenses against a teacher who knows all the answers.

IT therefore becomes necessary to see what sort of being the Japanese teacher is. Above all, he is likely to be a member of the Japan Teachers' Union. This organization claims a membership of more than 600,000, or some nine tenths of all the teachers in Japan, excluding university teachers but including part-time teachers on the lower levels. Though the claim is probably exaggerated, even enemies of the Teachers' Union concede that at least two thirds of the teachers in Japan, high school and lower, belong to it. No other teachers' organization is anywhere near as large.

There is no mystery about what the Teachers' Union stands for, because it has set forth its aims in its platform, "An Outline of a Teacher's Ethics," drafted in 1951 and still in effect. This is a remarkable document. It begins with the general view of the U.S. Education Mission to the effect that moral principles are derived from concrete situations, and then it proceeds in the most doctrinaire fashion imaginable to lay down absolute principles. Teachers, says the outline, are members of the working class. Their assigned position is the schoolroom, and there they must further the class struggle. "Eighteenth Century individualism" is not sufficient to the needs of our time (this theme is repeated over and over again). And so on.

FROM the international point of view, the most significant part of the document is that which outlines the views of the Teachers' Union on maintaining peace. The world conflict is seen as one between "capitalism" (not democracy, it is important to note) and communism. That conflict, says the union, is a problem for the United States and the U.S.S.R. to solve, and one in which Japan should not allow itself to become involved. But the sympathies of the union soon become clear, as do its views on who is to blame for unpleasant tensions in the world. "Peace is what the people want, but the capitalists do not make money from peace, and so they see it as a terrible threat to them. No doubt it is. Such is the fatal cancer in the capitalist system. . . . Those who instinctively think peace a threat to them—that is, the capitalists—must now be attacked and thrown out as miscreants who incite the people to war."

This document was written while the Occupation was still in control of Japan. If it provides the ideological equipment with which several hundred thousand teachers face up to their duties, then a peculiar sort of world will be taking shape in the mind of young Japan. War is the great evil, and the causes of war are simple: capitalists cause war, and the United States is a capitalist state. There is no room for the American notion that the West is defending not capitalism but democracy.

It is alarming to try to imagine what will happen when the twigs bent today by "social studies" are large enough to blot out the sun. But perhaps one need not despair. The reasons for a teacher's belonging to the union are varied,

and the mere fact that he belongs does not mean that he is under its influence. He has been subjected over the years to the indoctrination of the union, to be sure, and he has done little to challenge its authority. When the union has its annual convention and the time comes for electing officers, the Japanese newspapers regularly carry headlines suggesting that it is about to split wide open. Yet to the outsider the choice seems to be meaningless. There is no effective opposition faction that seeks to remake the union into a nonpolitical vocational organization.

But despite the union's power to apply social sanctions and its rather cruel willingness to harass defectors, there have been defections. Moreover, the union may not have quite the control over its members that pessimists think it has. After the government's decision in 1957 to establish nationwide teacher ratings, the union tried to turn out the nation's teachers in one massive phalanx of resistance. The move failed.

WHATEVER its defects, the school system gives almost every Japanese the ability to read if he so wishes. Journalism and the publishing business in turn give him an enormous amount of reading material to choose from. Seldom was a country more richly supplied with printed words than Japan is today.

Every month the supply of books becomes richer by something like 2,000 titles, and every week a flood of magazines burdens the National Railways. The total number of magazines dumped upon the newsstands has run as high as 12 or 13 million a week. *Bungei Shunjū*, the biggest of the higher-brow monthlies, has an estimated circulation of half a million.

Japan is a paradise for the free-lance journalist and the popular writer. There is a most prosperous class of the former, who are prepared to offer an opinion on anything. As for popular writers, the declared incomes of the most famous run four or five times as high as those of the best-paid baseball players, and it is a very rare movie star who does as well. The output of the more prolific writers is staggering. Sometimes they have a number of serials running simultaneously in newspapers and magazines. When a writer has made his name, his great problem, if he wishes to maintain any literary standard, is to keep from writing too much.

The weekly magazines go in for sex and crime, and a strong antiforeign strain runs through them. They are never happier than when their lurid tales involve that most corrupt institution, the foreign community of Tokyo. The strain persists even on the higher journalistic levels. *Bungei Shunjū*, which is probably the most influential magazine in Japan, recently carried a very successful series of articles which sought to implicate Americans in a number of cruel and mysterious incidents. These included the shooting of a police inspector, the murder of the president of the National Railways, the poisoning of a dozen bank employees and the crash of a civil airliner.

Dominating the rarefied upper reaches of journalism and publishing is an institution with a following so devoted, especially among the young, that its admirers might almost be called a religious congregation: the Iwanami Publishing Company. It is a mark of belonging to the intelligentsia for a young person to have an Iwanami book or magazine showing somewhere on his person. Much of Iwanami's prestige derives from its reputation as a publisher of solid, scholarly works. But its magazines and soft-cover books are generally far to the Left. *Sekai*, the principal Iwanami monthly magazine, has a distinct fondness for The New China, the Soviet Union and Fidel Castro. In the book field, the best-seller lists are never without titles from the Iwanami paperback series, whose political orientation is similar to that of the magazine.

BESIDES books and magazines, the Japanese reading public has newspapers in overwhelming supply. Total daily circulation is 24 million, or, if morning and evening papers with the same name are counted separately, 36 million. Far more than American ones do, Japanese papers depend upon circulation for income. The biggest newspapers are among the best in the country. The largest and most influential of

all, *Asahi*, claims a nationwide circulation of some five million, and it would be on anyone's list of the four or five best in the country.

Japanese newspapers are technically impressive. The difficulties of transmitting the Japanese written language have been overcome with the most remarkable ingenuity. Teleprinters are in operation which can handle both the Roman alphabet and Sino-Japanese characters. In 1959, *Asahi* became the first newspaper in the world to make printing plates, on a commercial basis, directly from facsimile transmission of complete news pages. The method is in use for the paper's far northern edition.

By journalistic standards rather than engineering ones, however, the biggest Japanese papers are not quite up to the world's best. They are wanting in what might be called integrity—and by this it is meant not that they are dishonest but that they fail to add up to anything unified and complete. The various departments seem to go their own ways, so that on a given day an editorial will be advising caution and "self-reflection" on some problem or other, while the literary page will be demanding immediate action on the same problem, and the back pages will be in effect inciting to riot.

THERE seem to be many causes for this confusing state of affairs: a reluctance on the part of the top editors to sit down hard on subordinates, however inferior their rank, who have ideas of their own; the work of pressure groups whose activities infringe on editorial prerogatives; and the neutral poses adopted by most of the big newspapers, which in theory refuse to take sides in political controversies. In practice this means that the various parts of the papers are free to take what sides they will, and the viewpoints represented in any one newspaper often seem to cancel each other out.

As for the pressure groups, their influence is leftist. Chief among them is the Shimbun Rōren or Federation of Newspaper Workers, which is affiliated with the Marxist Sōhyō labor federation. The Shimbun Rōren controls virtually the whole labor force of the biggest dailies, *Asahi* and *Mainichi*, including editorial staffs up to the rank of assistant desk man.

The Shimbun Rōren's aims are partly political. Its attitudes recently caused the Newspaper Publishers' Association to complain as follows:

"Times have changed, and restrictions today come not necessarily from above. Against those from below, a free press has almost no legal defenses. . . . On all sorts of pretexts, unions continue to interfere with editorial rights. A major reason is that Sōhyō, to which the Shimbun Rōren belongs, has departed from the prime function of the labor movement, to improve the economic position of the worker, and has launched out on excessively political activities. It has, for instance, mobilized its unions toward such political ends as preventing amendment of . . . the Security Treaty with the United States. . . . It has attempted to make its position reflected in editorial policies."

WHETHER or not the Shimbun Rōren can claim full credit, the tone of the news stories in the biggest papers was noticeably partial to the forces opposing the Security Treaty with the U.S. in 1960. Headlines of the time suggest that sensational newspaper coverage helped a great deal to keep the disturbances going—indeed, that important sections of the press were intent upon keeping things going. Even while the editorial writers were urging quiet reflection and cautioning against violence, the news columns were wildly beating the drum. The size of the demonstrations was consistently exaggerated. The figures released by the demonstrators appeared prominently in the headlines, while those released by the police, which were only a fraction as high, were buried. During the lull following one demonstration the headlines would commence building up for the next. When a girl student was killed on June 15, the newspapers were maudlin. Wholly unwarranted publicity was given to the theory that the police strangled her or clubbed her to death. In short, some of the best papers in Japan were irresponsible.

Zenrō, the anti-Sōhyō labor federation, has accused the Shimbun Rōren of persuading its members to distort the news in the bitter Miike coal strike of 1959–1960. The strictures of Zenrō and the Newspaper Publishers' Association would perhaps not be entirely convincing were it not for the fact that one important organization of journalists—the Japan Congress of Journalists—has publicly boasted of its success in giving the papers an anti-treaty bias. The congress has a membership in excess of 1,500 and is strong in *Asahi*, the Iwanami Publishing Company and the Kyōdō News Service (the principal supplier of news to the provincial press). It works closely with the Communist-dominated International Organization of Journalists.

AS matters stand today, then, one may expect that energetic and able elements in the newspaper world, taking advantage of weak editorial control, will build up a sense of crisis whenever something new develops in relations with the United States, and will inflate any incident to the utmost.

Yet, as with Japanese teachers and their union, the situation is not wholly black. The publishers' statement already quoted is evidence that editors may be awakening to their responsibilities. On October 7, 1960, *Asahi* carried a long and moving article by its managing editor on the struggle to keep news reporting honest. The article was concerned largely with pressure from the Left during the anti-treaty disturbances.

It is worth noting, too, that advertising is becoming more important in the journalistic world. Circulation is at the saturation point, but total advertising space in the first quarter of 1959 went up 17 per cent over 1958. Perhaps, as papers come to depend on something besides a titillated and agitated mass following, they will find it necessary to have principles, and principles that do not imply tearing society apart. To Americans, the notion of successful pressure on a newspaper by its advertisers may seem repellent. But the reader of the Japanese press finds himself occasionally thinking that almost any influence would be welcome if it were to stimulate a few important newspapers into a search for the integrity that has until now been lacking.

First grade pupils at the Showa Primary School in Tokyo join in a reading drill. Intensive teaching gives Japan a high literacy rate

A Testing Time for Changes in Learning

The educational reforms of the Occupation had many aims, but among the most important were the replacing of unquestioning acceptance of authority with thorough training in citizenship, the granting of equal status to girls and the broadening of opportunities for higher education. The results are still extremely speculative, though a promising start has been made. Japan has no lack of educational administrators, but there is a severe shortage of first-rate teachers.

AT HIGH SCHOOL, *girls have been given greater opportunities for advancing their studies, thereby opening up a whole new world for themselves*

DRAMA GROUP at Tokyo's Hakuo High School rehearses parts for a play. Boys and girls join in many other club activities, including dancing and journalism.

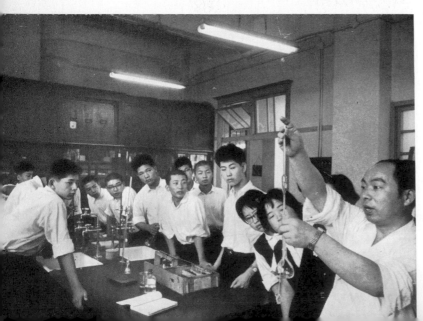

CHEMISTRY CLASS watches its instructor conduct an experiment (*left*). Technical progress has created a growing need for services of skilled women in industry.

FIELD TRIP to the Diet gives a high school social studies class an eyewitness view of the workings of democratic government from the visitors' gallery of the Lower House. Such an excursion is a novelty, particularly for the girls, since Japanese women played no part in politics until 1946, when they first got the vote.

COLLEGE LIFE *is a time of anxiety. Competition for entry is acute and academic success is difficult to achieve*

TENSE STUDENTS (*left*) crowd around an official notice board at a university in Tokyo to find out the results of examinations which will determine their future.

LEISURE HOURS bring students to the Tokyo municipal swimming pool (*opposite*), which is part of a vast complex of new buildings for a variety of sports events.

DILIGENT SCHOLARS at the Aoyama Gakuin University (*below*) cram for tests and quiz one another. This Tokyo institution is well known for its English studies.

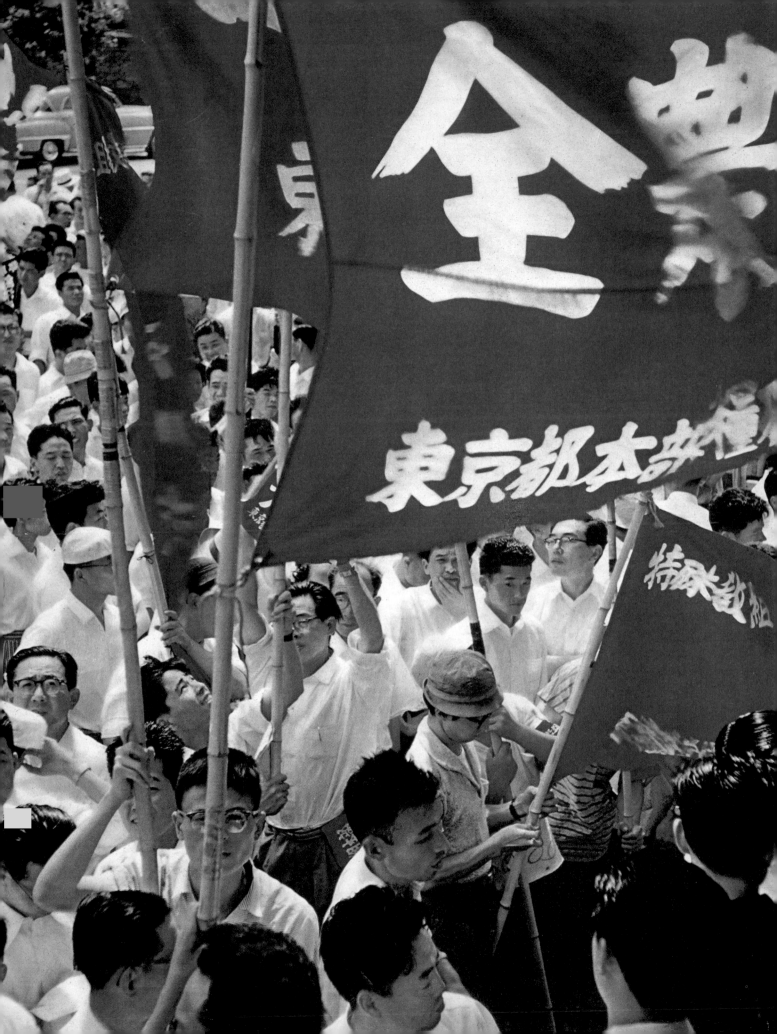

10

A Nation in the Balance

THERE is an imaginary border line skirting
the ridges of Tokyo, which thrust eastward
toward the bay like fingers. In the days when
the city's predecessor, Edo, was a fishing village, the ridges came down to the water's edge.
The shogunate later filled in the shallow fringes
of the bay to provide a mercantile center for
the city and a place for the merchants to live.
The line between the eastern "downtown" of
the flats and the western "uptown" of the ridges
therefore became the line between the easygoing, slangy, pleasure-loving townsmen and the
austere members of the warrior class. Today it
may be taken to symbolize the political division
of the country.

East of the line, in the flats, is the world of
the Japanese who works hard, does not trouble
himself much with transcendental thoughts and
loves to have a festival now and then. Although
he may not be deliriously happy with things as

they are, he generally accepts them. In the hills to the west is the world of the professional and white-collar classes, of commuter trains, drab middle-class housing, the huge Iwanami Publishing Company and the influential and somewhat truculent *Asahi* newspaper. Suspicious of the West and badly informed about the realities of the Communist bloc, this is the articulate half of the country, and it can be relied on for opposition to anything asked of the Japanese—from enlarging an air base to sending a box of crackers to Laos—that makes the American alliance a real partnership. It is not from the poor low-lying districts east of the imaginary line but rather from the hilly white-collar districts to the west that Communists are elected to the Tokyo City Council.

Badly divided, with one half willing to accept fundamental principles that the other half wants only to turn upside down, Japan finds it difficult to come forward as a nation and answer the question that is put to it: Which side is it on?

The Japanese should not be pushed for an answer, but they may not be ignored. They have accomplished too much during the last century and particularly the last decade, and their position in the world is too important. Until a few years ago, Japan's economic stability was heavily dependent on the American economy. Today the dependence has been so reduced that some economists think Japan could weather a fairly severe American recession, though not a full-scale depression. If the resourcefulness of the Japanese stays with them, even the rising monster across the China Sea need not be as threatening a competitor as one might think it.

THE Japanese economy is one of the half dozen most powerful in the world. Any sudden transfer of such an economy to the other side in the cold war would be an event of tremendous moment. By tipping a delicate balance, it could, indeed, be the jolt that would send the whole precarious complex of world politics crashing into a final disaster.

Of all the great industrialized peoples of the world, the Japanese are the least committed, and so perhaps among those most strategically placed for administering that final push. It could be argued that France, with its own kind of polarization and its disaffected intellectuals, is in an equally good position; but when the French underwent a crisis in 1958, they turned for help not to a Marxist but to a conservative and a Catholic, General de Gaulle, and so back to the very sources of the western tradition. A shift to the other side would be for them a shattering revolution.

For the Japanese, a shift might bring cruelty and suffering later, but at the outset they would negotiate the change with little difficulty. With all allowances for the fact that in 1950 Japan was an occupied country, it was ominous that during the Korean War, when the United Nations forces seemed about to be pushed from the southeast corner of Korea, the Japanese Foreign Office remained silent. The question arose: Were responsible officials in Japan preparing to make the shift?

IT is difficult to blame the Japanese for this lack of firmness. They are part of the western alliance not because they are part of its tradition but because they lost a war with its strongest member. Material prosperity has not ended a feeling of restlessness. No number of washing machines can really substitute for a sense of mission. A person must belong to something, and postwar Japan has been so unsuccessful at defining what it is and what it is up to that it offers little with which a person can identify himself. Many Japanese—in a general way, those from east of the symbolic Tokyo line—are able to sink themselves into their work and so to accept the chiefly negative attractions of the American alliance. Others look to an "Afro-Asian bloc," which scarcely exists as a viable unit, and to a "Socialist bloc" (the Communist world), about which most of them are not well informed.

United only in a fear of war and the atom bomb, to which they alone have offered victims, the Japanese are in a difficult position. The observer pities a country that cannot make up its mind to defend itself but cannot really make up its mind to have others defend it; that cannot live with armaments (especially nuclear ones) but cannot live without them. The observer can even understand, so emotion-ridden is the question, why those who resolve the dilemma by airily dismissing defenses and defenders show a strong tendency to try to eat their cake and have it too.

It is the articulate intelligentsia that does so, and in a way this is a new twist to the venerable Japanese institution of blithely accepting contradictory beliefs. The policy approved by the intelligentsia means, in effect, that a country can have security without paying for it. The policy in question is disarmed neutralism, and it has the support of the second largest party in the country, the Socialist party.

There are two cynical but logical ways of defending such a policy. One is the position of the few who have followed their Marxist assumptions through to a conclusion: that neutralism is a device for preparing to switch sides in the world conflict. The other is the hardheaded position held by such operators as President Gamal Abdel Nasser of Egypt: that the two sides can be played off against each other.

For most of its supporters, however, disarmed neutralism is a matter of wishfulness and self-deception. It assumes that a large and economically powerful country, situated far from the nearest help, would be safe if disarmed, because any invasion or fifth-column subversion would start a major war. In other words, it assumes that the United States, even if it were restricted to its own side of the Pacific, would come to the aid of the Japanese in an attack. Hence a self-deception arises that verges on willful duplicity: the West is simultaneously condemned and looked to for protection.

YET intolerable though the relationship may seem to an American, it is after all the one in which a parent generally stands to a child and, by extension, a stronger country may expect to stand to a weaker. The stronger party must accept it in good humor and hope that there will one day be an awakening. Americans have

an added reason to be patient. The attitude of Japan toward the United States is reminiscent of the 19th Century, when a favorite American pastime was twisting the British lion's tail, even though America's luxury of disarmed neutrality at that time was essentially dependent on British naval power.

And there is a more practical reason for American forbearance. Even if the child seems excessively annoying and selfish, he should not be encouraged to run away, for he is quite capable of setting fire to the house.

THE chances of an awakening cannot be described as good. Yet they exist. Though it is still far from victory, the Socialist party creeps a little closer with every election. In its eagerness to make the last push, it may turn to wooing the essentially conservative voter east of that imaginary downtown-uptown line. It cannot do so unless it stops talking revolution, divests itself of Marxist trappings and tones down its hostility toward the United States, a country that continues to be popular east of the line. Late in 1960 the party began talking about something called "structural reform," which perhaps offers hope. So far the talk has been ambiguous, with one clause contradicting the next in the same sentence. The whole argument leads to the general but somewhat puzzling conclusion that there will and again there will not be a revolution.

Possibly the Socialist party is trying to hint, by ways of its own, that its theoretical base will continue to be Marxist—for the power of the labor unions demands it—but that there is no need to be greatly worried. But on that, one can only speculate, wait and hope—and add that if the Socialists expect to come into power by legal means, if they want to speed up the process and if they are not relying on economic disaster to do their work for them, they will have to make some such accommodation.

The Socialist party is one of the more puzzling elements in a frequently bewildering country. It is a very Japanese phenomenon, one which the Japanese must be left to take care of.

But if the West, particularly the United States, cannot influence this situation, the reverse is also true to some extent: there are many things shaping the future of Japan that are quite out of Japanese hands. This can be said of any country, but it is particularly true of a country that cannot make up its mind about what it is and where it is going. What it cannot decide for itself, someone else must decide for it.

For the West, and particularly its most powerful nation, a pair of injunctions would seem to be an apt conclusion to what has been said: Be quiet, and be strong.

BE quiet. If the troubles the United States had with Japan in 1960 taught a lesson, it was that the Japanese must not be pushed to a decision about their responsibilities in the world. They may eventually come to a decision by their own devices, but as things stand today nothing should be done that might cause a debate on the fundamentals of foreign policy. Even concessions to the Japanese are likely to provoke such a debate, which becomes a debate less about the concessions than about whether the American alliance itself should be permitted. No conclusion to the debate seems possible at the moment, and the fear and frustration it produces are likely in their turn to produce violence.

Proposals which demand of the Japanese more positive cooperation than they are now offering are still more dangerous. It may seem that every nation has an obligation to defend itself, particularly if in relative terms its financial situation is improving while that of its chief ally is declining. Yet the Japanese are too important to the western world and too vulnerable to be left wandering unprotected, and they seem absolutely unwilling to protect themselves. For this reluctance the United States must carry a large share of the blame. Any proposal for adequate defenses flies squarely in the face of the American-drafted Japanese Constitution, and any attempt to amend the Constitution would provoke an opposition so violent that it would verge on armed rebellion. So the disagreeable but undeniable situation, not likely to change

for a long time, is that the United States must be responsible for the defense of Japan, and can expect little in return except vituperation.

And the United States and the West must be strong. There is yet another important element in Japanese neutralism. In addition to being in some measure cynical, in some measure pro-Communist and in some measure wishful, neutralism is based on fear and opportunism, in this case closely intertwined. There are Japanese who simply want to be on the winning side, and they think they see which side it will be. Hence, whether or not they have any convictions, they say favorable things about China.

It is possible to understand and even to sympathize with such people. The United States is across the Pacific, but the Soviet Union is within sight of the northernmost Japanese island, and the so-called "missile gap" between the United States and the U.S.S.R. has been deeply impressed upon the Japanese consciousness. Even if the sympathies of a particular Japanese are with the West, he knows that his children are in Japan, and he would not like to see them deported to Siberia because of his desire merely to say what he thinks.

FOR the United States and the West, the obvious course is to show that the other side is not going to win. Saber rattling will not help. It will merely confirm the views of many Japanese on the "capitalist" origins of war. A clear show that the West has not backed out of the race, on the other hand, could help a great deal.

On a practical level, the strength of the American economy is important. Although Japan is not as dependent on the United States as it once was, it is nevertheless more dependent on the United States than on any other country.

A serious recession in America is the thing most certain to disturb the solid voting habits of the Japanese. To remain prosperous is perhaps the best thing the United States and the West can do for Japan. Economic stability may not answer all the questions, but economic disaster would be quite certain to produce all the wrong answers.

Students browse intently in a busy Tokyo bookshop. Next page: A politician harangues street crowds during an election campaign

SEARCHING *for wider knowledge and yearning for a better life . . .*

. . . the people of Japan approach a critical point in their history. Although

they attempt to determine the future, events may prove beyond their control

Appendix

HISTORICAL DATES

B.C.

660 Founding of the Japanese Empire by Emperor Jimmu

A.D.

200 Korean expedition of Empress Jingo

284 Japanese court sends to Paikche (Korea) for scribe Wani. Official adoption of Chinese script follows

552 Paikche sends Japan image of Buddha, volumes of the scriptures and, in 554, men learned in the classics, medicine and other scholarly fields

646 Taikwa reform edict is formulated, applying to Japan the centralized bureaucratic system of the Chinese Empire

710 Nara, first permanent capital, is laid out on model of the Chinese capital

741 Buddhism becomes in effect the state religion

794 After 10 years of building a new capital at Nagaoka, Emperor Kwammu switches to Kyoto, five miles distant, and rebuilds his capital there

1185 Struggle between Taira and Minamoto clans, which ends in victory for the Minamoto. Epic period in Japanese history. Formation of samurai caste

1192 Yoritomo becomes first shogun; sets up *bakufu* (military headquarters) at Kamakura, in eastern Japan

1199 Hojo regency begins on death of Yoritomo

1219 Fujiwara puppet shogun set up in Kamakura

1274 First invasion of Japan by Kublai Khan, Mongol ruler of China

1281 Second Mongol invasion

1333 Emperor Go-Daigo destroys Kamakura. Hojo regency ends with suicide of last regent

1336 Rival courts: Go-Daigo establishes "Southern" court; Ashikaga Takauji sets up Emperor Komyo in Kyoto

1392 Half-century struggle over succession—fundamentally a redistribution of feudal power—ends with Ashikaga supremacy

467–1477 Feudal Wars of Onin. Many families destroyed

1477 Collapse of central government as result of civil war. Ashikaga shoguns powerless. Imperial house penniless

1500 Whole of Japan at war. Many peasant uprisings

1542 First major contact with the West: three Portuguese sailors shipwrecked. Traders and Jesuit priests follow

1549 Spanish missionary St. Francis Xavier reaches Japan

1568 Nobunaga becomes *de facto* shogun. End of Ashikaga power

1571 Nobunaga destroys warlike monasteries and crushes Buddhism as a political force

1582 Hideyoshi succeeds Nobunaga and imposes peace

1587 First persecution of Christians

1592 Unsuccessful Korean expedition, terminated in 1598 by death of Hideyoshi

1597 Second Korean expedition

1598 Ieyasu, founder of Tokugawa family, succeeds Hideyoshi

1600 Battle of Sekigahara won by Ieyasu against rebel chiefs. Edo, later called Tokyo, becomes country's administrative capital. Ieyasu becomes shogun

1615 Ieyasu becomes master of Japan by victory at Osaka Castle

1622–1651 Zenith of feudal institutions under third Tokugawa shogun, Iemitsu

1624 Expulsion of the Spaniards. Increasing antiforeign feeling

1637 Drastic antiforeign and anti-Christian edict. Shimabara rebellion, caused primarily by agrarian troubles but given moral impetus by Christianity, leads to expulsion of Portuguese and closure of country to foreign influence

1657 Great fire in Edo

1716 Increased pressure from changing economic conditions. Yoshimune, an enlightened shogun, tries to remedy desperate situation by a "back to Ieyasu" program

1783–1787 Rice riots. Growing opposition to the shogunate

1838 Famines. Financial embarrassment of shogunate. General economic collapse threatened

1853–1854 Perry's "black ships" arrive. First treaty with U.S. signed

1858 Commercial treaty with U.S. signed without emperor's sanction. Opposition to shogunate foments antiforeign demonstrations in which "outside lords," especially of Satsuma and Choshu, are leaders

1863 Reprisal bombardment of Kagoshima, capital of Satsuma clan, by British fleet. American, Dutch and French vessels fired on by Choshu forts at Shimonoseki

1864 Reprisal movement of four powers. Choshu forts destroyed by allied squadron of Dutch, French and British ships

1867–1868 Shogunate overthrown. "Restoration" of power to emperor. Mutsuhito accedes as Emperor Meiji; moves imperial court to Edo, naming it Tokyo (Eastern Capital)

1869 Chiefs of the four great clans (Satsuma, Choshu, Tosa and Hizen) surrender their fiefs to the emperor. Clan heads made governors of former provinces

1871 Second reorganization. System of local autonomy abolished. Disestablishment of the samurai

1874 First popular assembly. Alliance between government and Mitsubishi interests for punitive expedition against Formosa

1876 Samurai forbidden to wear two swords. Conscript army of all classes set up. Dissatisfaction of samurai culminates in the Satsuma rebellion, "not against the emperor but against his evil counselors"

1889 Constitution (drafted by Prince Ito, on German model) "solemnly promulgated." Imperial Diet opened in 1890

1894–1895 Sino-Japanese War, won by the Japanese

1904–1905 Russo-Japanese War, won by the Japanese

1910 Korea annexed to Japan by imperial rescript

1912 End of Meiji reign. Accession of Yoshihito

1914 Japan enters World War I on the side of the Allies

1921 Incapacity of Yoshihito. Regency of Hirohito

1923 Great Earthquake destroys much of Tokyo

1924 U.S. Congress passes exclusion law aimed at the Japanese

1926 Death of Emperor Yoshihito. The Showa period begins with Emperor Hirohito

1931 The "Manchurian Adventure"

1933 Japan withdraws from League of Nations

1936 Top government officials assassinated by army extremists. New cabinet dominated by military

1937 War opens with China. Sacking of Nanking

1940 Japan concludes alliance with Germany and Italy

1941–1945 War with the United States, Britain and the Netherlands

1945–1952 U.S. Occupation regime

1952 Treaty of San Francisco restores Japanese independence

FOR FURTHER READING

CHAPTERS 1, 5: JAPAN TODAY (GENERAL)

Beardsley, Richard K., *Village Japan*. University of Chicago Press, 1959.

Benedict, Ruth, *The Chrysanthemum and the Sword*. Houghton Mifflin, 1946.

Chamberlain, Basil Hall, *Things Japanese*. Thompson, Kobe, 1939.

Cressey, George B., *Asia's Lands and Peoples*. McGraw-Hill, 1951.

Dore, R. P., *City Life in Japan*. Routledge & Kegan Paul, London, 1958.

Embree, John F., *The Japanese Nation; A Social Survey*. Farrar & Rinehart, 1945.

Enright, D. J., *The World of Dew; Aspects of Living Japan*. Charles E. Tuttle, Tokyo, 1956.

Gibney, Frank, *Five Gentlemen of Japan*. Farrar, Straus, and Young, 1953.

Hearn, Lafcadio, *Japan; An Attempt at Interpretation*. Charles E. Tuttle, Tokyo, 1955.

Kawasaki, Ichiro, *The Japanese Are Like That*. Charles E. Tuttle, 1955.

Keene, Donald, *Living Japan*. Doubleday, 1959.

Maraini, Fosco, *Meeting with Japan*. Viking Press, 1960.

Moloney, Dr. James Clark, *Understanding the Japanese Mind*. Philosophical Library, 1954.

Ogrizek, Doré, ed., *Japan*. McGraw-Hill, 1957.

Simpson, Colin, *Japan; An Intimate View*. A. S. Barnes, 1959.

Vining, Elizabeth Gray, *Windows for the Crown Prince*. J. B. Lippincott, 1952.

Webb, Herschel, *An Introduction to Japan*. Columbia University Press, 1957.

CHAPTER 2: HISTORY

Borton, Hugh, *Japan's Modern Century*. Ronald Press, 1955. *Japan Since 1931; Its Political and Social Development*. Institute of Pacific Relations, 1940.

Boxer, C. R., *The Christian Century in Japan, 1549–1650*. University of California Press, 1951.

Cosenza, M. E., ed., *The Complete Journal of Townsend Harris*. Charles E. Tuttle, 1959.

Ike, Nobutake, *The Beginnings of Political Democracy in Japan*. Johns Hopkins Press, 1950.

Maki, John M., *Japanese Militarism; Its Cause and Cure*. Alfred A. Knopf, 1945.

Reischauer, Edwin O., *Japan; Past and Present*. Alfred A. Knopf, 1953. *The United States and Japan*. Harvard University Press, 1957.

Reischauer, Robert Karl, *Japan; Government-Politics*. Thomas Nelson & Sons, 1939.

Sansom, George B., *A History of Japan to 1334*. Stanford University Press, 1958. *Japan; A Short Cultural History*. D. Appleton-Century, 1943. *The Western World and Japan*. Alfred A. Knopf, 1950.

Scalapino, Robert A., *Democracy and the Party Movement in Prewar Japan*. University of California Press, 1953.

Storry, Richard, *A History of Modern Japan*. Penguin Books, 1960. *The Double Patriots; A Study of Japanese Nationalism*. Houghton Mifflin, 1957.

Tsunoda, Ryusaku, W.T. de Bary and Donald Keene, eds., *Sources of Japanese Tradition*. Columbia University Press, 1958.

Walworth, Arthur, *Black Ships off Japan; The Story of Commodore Perry's Expedition*. Alfred A. Knopf, 1946.

Yanaga, Chitoshi, *Japan Since Perry*. McGraw-Hill, 1949.

CHAPTER 3: POLITICS SINCE THE WAR

Ball, William Macmahon, *Japan; Enemy or Ally?* Institute of Pacific Relations, 1949.

Bisson, Thomas Arthur, *Prospects for Democracy in Japan*. Institute of Pacific Relations, 1949.

Brown, Delmer M., *Nationalism in Japan*. University of California Press, 1955.

Colbert, Evelyn S., *The Left Wing in Japanese Politics*. Institute of Pacific Relations, 1952.

Dore, R. P., *Land Reform in Japan*. Oxford University Press, 1959.

Ike Nobutake, *Japanese Politics; An Introductory Survey*. Alfred A. Knopf, 1957.

Kawai, Kazuo, *Japan's American Interlude*. University of Chicago Press, 1960.

Morris, Ivan, *Nationalism and the Right Wing in Japan*. Oxford University Press, 1960.

Quigley, Harold S., and John E. Turner, *The New Japan; Government and Politics*. University of Minnesota Press, 1956.

Shigemitsu, Mamoru, *Japan and Her Destiny*. E. P. Dutton, 1958.

Swearingen, Roger, and Paul Langer, *Red Flag in Japan*. Harvard University Press, 1952.

Wildes, Harry Emerson, *Typhoon in Tokyo; The Occupation and Its Aftermath*. Macmillan, 1954.

Yanaga, Chitoshi, *Japanese People and Politics*. John Wiley & Sons, 1956.

CHAPTER 4: THE ECONOMY

Ackerman, Edward A., *Japan's Natural Resources and Their Relation to Japan's Economic Future*. University of Chicago Press, 1953.

Allen, George C., *A Short Economic History of Modern Japan, 1867–1937*. George Allen & Unwin, London, 1951. *Japan's Economic Recovery*. Oxford University Press, 1958.

Bisson, Thomas Arthur, *Japan's War Economy*. Institute of Pacific Relations, 1945.

Cohen, Jerome B., *Japan's Economy in War and Reconstruction*. University of Minnesota Press, 1949. *Japan's Postwar Economy*. Indiana University Press, 1958.

CHAPTER 6: ARTS AND LETTERS

Blyth, R. H., *Haiku*. Hokuseido, Tokyo, 1952.

Bowers, Faubion, *Japanese Theatre*. Hermitage House, 1952.

Bowie, Henry P., *On the Laws of Japanese Painting*. Dover Publications, 1951.

Drexler, Arthur, *The Architecture of Japan*. Museum of Modern Art, 1955.

Ernst, Earle, *The Kabuki Theatre*. Oxford University Press, 1956.

Keene, Donald, ed., *Anthology of Japanese Literature*. Grove Press, 1955. *Japanese Literature*. Grove Press, 1955. *Modern Japanese Literature*. Grove Press, 1956.

Michener, James A., *The Floating World*. Random House, 1954. *The Hokusai Sketch-Books; Selections from the Manga*. Charles E. Tuttle, 1958.

Munsterberg, Hugo, *The Folk Arts of Japan*. Charles E. Tuttle, 1958.

Paine, Robert Treat, and Alexander Soper, *The Art and Architecture of Japan*. Penguin Books, 1955.

Sitwell, Sacheverell, *The Bridge of the Brocade Sash*. World Publishing, 1959.

Terry, Charles S., ed., *Masterworks of Japanese Art*. Charles E. Tuttle, 1956.

Waley, Arthur, *The Nō Plays of Japan*. Grove Press, 1954.

Warner, Langdon, *The Enduring Art of Japan*. Harvard University Press, 1952.

Yoshida, Tetsuro, *The Japanese House and Garden*. Frederick A. Praeger, 1955.

CHAPTER 7: ENTERTAINMENT AND SPORTS

Anderson, Joseph I., and Donald Richie, *The Japanese Film*. Charles E. Tuttle, 1959.

Kato, Hidetoshi, ed., *Japanese Popular Culture*. Charles E. Tuttle, 1958.

Malm, William P., *Japanese Music and Musical Instruments*. Charles E. Tuttle, 1959.

Mihori, Fukumensi, *Japanese Game of "Go"*. Japan Government Railways, Board of Tourist Industries booklet, 1939.

Sargent, J. A., *Sumo: The Sport and the Tradition*. Charles E. Tuttle, 1959.

Takagaki, Shinzo, and Harold E. Sharp, *The Techniques of Judo*. Charles E. Tuttle, 1957.

Tanabe, Hisao, *Japanese Music*. Kokusai Bunka Shinkokai, Tokyo, 1959.

Yamata, Kikou, *Three Geishas*. John Day, 1956.

CHAPTER 8: RELIGION AND FOLKLORE

Anezaki, Masaharu, *History of Japanese Religion*. Kegan Paul, Trench, Trubner, London, 1930.

Barrett, William, ed., *Zen Buddhism; Selected Writings of D. T. Suzuki*. Doubleday, 1956.

Bellah, Robert N., *Tokugawa Religion*. Free Press, 1957.

Bunce, William K., ed., *Religions in Japan; Buddhism, Shinto, Christianity*. Charles E. Tuttle, 1955.

Coomaraswamy, Ananda K., *Hinduism and Buddhism*. Philosophical Library, 1943.

Eliot, Sir Charles, *Japanese Buddhism*. Barnes & Noble, 1959.

Herrigel, Eugen, *Zen in the Art of Archery*. Pantheon, 1953.

Holtom, D.C., *Modern Japan and Shinto Nationalism.* University of Chicago Press, 1947.

Iglehart, Charles W., *A Century of Protestant Christianity in Japan.* Charles E. Tuttle, 1959.

Laures, Johannes, *Catholic Church in Japan.* Charles E. Tuttle (n.d.).

Nishida, Kitaro, *Intelligibility and the Philosophy of Nothingness.* Maruzen, Tokyo, 1958.

Nitobe, Inazo, *Bushidō; The Soul of Japan.* G. P. Putnam's Sons, 1905.

Ross, Nancy Wilson. *The World of Zen.* Random House, 1960.

Suzuki, Daisetz T., *Zen and Japanese Culture.* Pantheon, 1960.

Tsunoda, Ryusaku, W. T. de Bary and Donald Keene, eds., *Sources of Japanese Tradition.* Columbia University Press, 1958.

CHAPTER 9: EDUCATION AND JOURNALISM

Anderson, Ronald S., *Japan; Three Epochs of Modern Education.* U.S. Department of Health, Education and Welfare, 1959.

Education in Japan. Japanese Ministry of Education, 1959.

Report of the United States Education Mission to Japan. U.S. Department of State, 1946.

Sheba, Kimpei, *I Cover Japan.* Tokyo News Service, 1954.

CHAPTER 10: JAPAN'S WORLD POSITION

Borton, Hugh, and others, *Japan Between East and West.* Harper & Brothers, 1957.

Leng, Shao Chuan, *Japan and Communist China.* Institute of Pacific Relations, 1958.

Reischauer, Edwin O., *The United States and Japan.* Harvard University Press, 1957.

Schwantes, Robert S., *Japanese and Americans.* Council on Foreign Relations, 1955.

Strausz-Hupe, Robert, Alvin J. Cottrell and James E. Dougherty, eds., *American-Asian Tensions.* Frederick A. Praeger, 1956.

FAMOUS FIGURES AND WORKS IN JAPANESE CULTURE

In this list, proper names are written in the Japanese style: family name first, given name second.

ARCHAIC PERIOD   (Before 552 A.D.)

Sculpture: Ancient Shinto artifacts near burial mounds, in particular clay figurines known as *haniwa.*

ASUKA PERIOD   (552–645)

Architecture: The first surviving Buddhist temple, Hōryūji, near Nara.
Sculpture: Wooden and bronze sculpture of the Tori school.
Painting: Religious scenes on doors and panels of Tamamushi-zushi, a miniature shrine in the Hōryūji.

NARA PERIOD   (645–794)

Architecture: Building of monasteries. Tōshōdaiji, pagoda of Yakushiji.
Sculpture: Giant Buddhas in bronze, clay and hollow dry lacquer: bronze, 53'-high seated Buddha in the Tōdaiji at Nara; the thousand-armed Kannon of Tōshōdaiji.
Painting: Frescoes of Buddhist Paradise in the Hōryūji. *Sutras of Past and Present Karma,* oldest preserved scrolls.
Poetry: *Manyōshū (Collection of Myriad Leaves):* anthology of 4,500 Japanese poems, ranging from the *waka* in 31 syllables (alternating five- and seven-syllable lines) to *ehōka,* or "long poem," in more than 100 lines.
Prose: *Kojiki (Record of Ancient Matters)* in Japanese, *Nihon-shoki (Chronicles of Japan)* in Chinese: officially commissioned, myth-laden histories of Japan.

HEIAN PERIOD   (794–1185)

Architecture: *Shinden-zukuri,* building-and-garden complex. Phoenix Hall, Hōōdō, at Uji, near Kyoto. Five-storied pagoda at Daigoji, near Kyoto. Kasuga shrine at Nara.
Sculpture: Shaka and Kannon statues in the Murōji, near Nara. Rise of hereditary schools from Jōchō; Amida by Jōchō in Phoenix Hall. Eleven-headed Kannon in the Hokkeji.
Painting: Beginning of landscape painting. Mandalas, symbolic representations of the universe. Amida Buddha and bodhisattvas descending from heaven at the Kōya monastery on Mount Kōya.
    Calligraphy. Beginning of secular art in the *Yamato-e* (colored picture scrolls): *The Tale of Genji* scroll.
Poetry: *Kokinshū (Ancient and Modern Collection):* anthology of elegant and complex poetry written by aristocracy.
Prose: *Genji monogatari (The Tale of Genji)* by Lady Murasaki (c. 978–c. 1031): world's first great novel. *Makura no sōshi (Pillow-Book)* by Sei Shōnagon (c. 966–c. 1013): perceptive commentary on court life.

KAMAKURA PERIOD   (1185–1333)

Architecture: New style of Zen architecture: Nanzenji, Daitokuji, Kenninji, Tōfukuji and Myōshinji in Kyoto; Kenchōji and Engakuji in Kamakura.

Sculpture: Golden age of sculpture, beginning with Kokei: the bronze (42' 6" high) Amida Buddha at Kamakura; wooden religious images and portrait statues by Unkei and his school.

Painting: *E-makimono* (picture scrolls with narrative content): scrolls of lives of Buddhist saints; Heiji Monogatari scroll of the battle between the Taira and Minamoto families; Buddhist hand scroll of hungry ghosts; hand scroll of diseases. Portrait of Yoritomo. The Tosa school.

Poetry: *Shinkokinshū* (*New Ancient and Modern Collection*): includes outstanding *waka* by priest Saigyō (1118–1190).

Prose: Emphasis on military tales, theme of impermanence of all things, and use of symbolism as attempt to suggest eternal truths: *Heike monogatari* (*The Tale of Heiki*), anonymous; *Hōjōki* (*An Account of My Hut*) by Kamo no Chōmei.

MUROMACHI PERIOD   (1333–1568)

Architecture: Kinkakuji, Golden Pavilion; Ginkakuji, Silver Pavilion in Kyoto.

Painting: Josetsu, Shōbun, Sesshū and Sesson, masters of Zen-inspired black and white ink painting. The Kanō family.

Poetry and Drama: Nō dramas (developed from primitive song and dance playlets) by Kan'nami Kiyotsugu (1333–1384) and his son Seami Motokiyo (1363–1443). *Kyōgen* (comic interludes), employing popular language, intersperse Nō performances. *Waka* poetry gives rise to linked verse sequence (*renga*), first three lines of which become independent poem—*haiku*.

AZUCHI-MOMOYAMA PERIOD   (1568–1615)

Architecture: New type of castle architecture: Shirasagi (White Heron) castle in Himeji. *Chashitsu* (the teahouse).

Painting: Gold leaf screen and wall paintings by Hasegawa Tōhaku and Kanō Eitoku.

EDO OR TOKUGAWA PERIOD   (1615–1868)

Sculpture: Polychrome carvings of the Nikkō shrines.

Painting: Color prints by Harunobu, Kiyonaga, Utamaro, Sharaku, Hokusai, Hiroshige. Paintings, designs, lacquers and pottery of Ogata Kōrin. Honami Kōetsu, Tawaraya Sōtatsu, Kanō Tanyū. Maruyama Okyo, leader of the naturalistic school. Ike Taiga, leader of anti-naturalist school. Shiba Kōkan, Ikeno Taiga, Watanabe Kazan, early painters influenced by western art.

Craft: Pottery, brass and iron utensils, folk toys, fans, lacquer trays, *netsuke* (small carvings, usually in wood or ivory).

Poetry: Matsuo Bashō (1644–1694), Yosa Buson (1716–1781) and Kobayashi Issa (1763–1828), masters of *haiku*, which becomes important genre.

Prose: Novels to suit newly prominent commercial class: *Five Women Who Loved Love* and *The Japanese Family Storehouse* by Ihara Saikaku (1642–1693); *Hizakurige* by Jippensha Ikku (1766–1831).

Drama: New drama forms: *jōruri* (puppet theater) plays by Chikamatsu Monzaemon (1653–1725), Takeda Izumo (1691–1756) and Chikamatsu Hanji (1725–1783). Kabuki dramas with live actors, appropriating much of repertory of *jōruri* and Nō plays.

MEIJI AND MODERN PERIODS   (1868 to Present)

Poetry: Akiko Yosano (1878–1942), poetess of great emotional power. Sakutarō Hagiwara (1888–1942), first successful poet in colloquial Japanese. Takuboku Ishikawa (1885–1912), most popular modern *waka* poet.

Literary Criticism: *Essence of the Novel* by Shōyō Tsubouchi (1859–1935): influential in development of Japanese novel.

Prose: *The Drifting Cloud* by Shimei Futabatei (1864–1909): first modern Japanese novel in subject and style. *The Wild Goose* by Ogai Mori (1862–1922): realistic study of Meiji Period woman. *Kokoro* by Sōseki Natsume (1867–1916): introspective, philosophical fiction. *The Broken Commandment* by Tōson Shimazaki (1872–1943): social realism. *Han's Crime, At Kinosaki* by Naoya Shiga (1883–): mainly autobiographical fiction. *A Fool's Love, Some Prefer Nettles, The Makioka Sisters* by Junichirō Tanizaki (1886–): conflict in claims of East and West. *Rashōmon* by Ryūnosuke Akutagawa (1892–1927): morbid and satirical short stories. *The River Sumida* by Kafū Nagai (1897–): elegies for a changing Tokyo. *The Dancing Girl of Izu, Snow Country* by Yasumari Kawabata (1899–): psychological fiction. *The Temple of the Golden Pavilion, The Sound of Waves*, by Yukio Mishima (1925–): traditional themes in modern settings.

Drama: *The Madman on the Roof* by Kan Kikuchi (1888–1948): lyric, poetic fantasy. *Twilight Crane* by Junji Kinoshita (1914–): folklore turned into modern drama.

Credits

The sources for the illustrations in this book are shown below. Credits for pictures from left to right are separated by commas, top to bottom by dashes.

Cover—Ronny Jaques

8, 9—John Launois from Black Star

10—Calligraphy by Yasuo Inoue

17, 18, 19—Eliot Elisofon

20—John Launois from Black Star

21, 22, 23—Eliot Elisofon

24—William J. Sumits and Herbert Orth

31—Map by Matt Greene

34, 35—David Douglas Duncan courtesy Tokyo National Museum

36, 37—Culver Pictures, The Bettmann Archive

38, 39—bottom left: Paul Dorsey

40—J. R. Eyerman

41—Eikoh Hosoe from Birnback Publishing Service

42—John Dominis

50 through 55—John Dominis

56, 57—Yasushi Nagao for Mainichi Shimbun

58—Associated Press

59—Jun Miki

60—Ewing Krainin from Photo Researchers, Inc.

65—Map by Mary Suzuki

68—Margaret Bourke-White

69—John Launois from Black Star for TIME

70, 71, 72—John Launois from Black Star

73—Hank Simons from Photo Researchers, Inc.—Louis Renault from Photo Researchers, Inc.

74, 75—John Launois from Black Star for FORTUNE, Kihachi Komatsu

76, 77—John Launois from Black Star

82, 83—John Dominis

84—John Launois from Black Star

85—S. Imai

86 through 89—John Launois from Black Star

95, 96—John Launois from Black Star

97—David Douglas Duncan

98, 99—left: courtesy National Gallery of Art, Washington, D.C.; right: William J. Sumits and Herbert Orth

100, 101—left: William J. Sumits and Herbert Orth; right: courtesy National Gallery of Art, Washington, D.C.

102, 103—David Douglas Duncan

104—Jerry Cooke for SPORTS ILLUSTRATED

111—John Dominis

112—Marc Riboud from Magnum

113—Jerry Cooke for SPORTS ILLUSTRATED

114, 115—Eliot Elisofon

116—Cornell Capa from Magnum

117—Ronny Jaques

118, 119—Howard Sochurek

122—Map by Mary Suzuki

125—Horace Bristol

126—John Launois from Black Star

127—Louis Renault from Photo Researchers, Inc.

128, 129—Jun Miki

130, 131—Takahiro Ono

132, 133—Jun Miki

139—Eiichi Matsumoto for Asahi Shimbun

140, 141—John Dominis

142—Jacqueline Paul from Lensgroup—Toge Fujihara from Monkmeyer Press Photos

143—Ezra Stoller

144, 149—John Dominis

150, 151—Jun Miki

ACKNOWLEDGMENTS

The editors of this book are indebted to Donald Keene, Associate Professor of Japanese, Columbia University, and Eugene Langston of the Japan Society, both of whom read and commented in detail on the entire text.

Index

This symbol in front of a page number indicates a photograph or painting of the subject mentioned.

Advertising, newspaper, 138
Ainu, 14
Akihito, Crown Prince, 46, *59
Amida Buddha, 78, *99, 121
Annam, 29
Aoyama Gakuin University, *143
Appliances, ownership statistics on, 63
Archaic Period, 27
Architecture, 89, 91, 93; influence of, on home architecture, 94; western influence on, 94
Aristocracy, in early Japanese history, 26, 27, 28, 123
Army officers, 33
Art: Buddhist influence on, 27, 95; effect of isolation on, 32, 93; esthetic principles of, 91–92, 96; future of, 93; of Heian Period, 27, 92; performing, 89, 109–110; religious, 92, *99–103; use of color in, 92; western influences on, 93–94, 110. *See also* Architecture; Painting; Sculpture; Theater arts
Asahi, newspaper, 137, 138, 146
Asakusa festival, 124
Asanuma, Inejiro, *57
Ashikaga family, 28
Asia: Japanese economic invasion of, 29; Japan's role in, 44
Asuka, 27
Asuka Period, 27
Atom bomb: destruction of Hiroshima by, *40; protests against, 14, *84–85
Australia, 33
Azuchi-Momoyama Period, 27

Ballet, 110
Bank of Japan, 64
Baseball, 105, 107
Bashō, Matsuo, 91
Behavior. *See* Codes of behavior and ethics
Belgium, 13
Benkei, 28
Berlin, 80
Birth rate, 13
Biwa, Lake, 26
Bon festival, 121, 124
Book publishing, 133, 136, 137
Buddha, 121. *See also* Amida Buddha
Buddhism: ceremonies and festivals of, 120–121, 124, *128–131; and Confucianism, 123; essence of, 77–78, 121; founding of, 121; history of, in Japan, 123; importation of, to Japan, 26, 27, 121; influence of, on art, 27, 95; medieval, 77–78, 123; number of followers of, 119; portrayal of deities

of, *99–100, 102; and Shinto, 119, 123; shrines, *map* 122; and suicide, 80. *See also* Zen Buddhism
Budget, average family, *chart* 62
Bungei Shunjū, magazine, 136, 137
Bunraku drama, *117

Calligraphy, oriental, 92
Cambodia, 29
Capital, Japanese: moves of, in early history, 26; Tokyo chosen as, 32
Castro, Fidel, 137
Catholicism in Japan, 30. *See also* Christianity
Chamberlain, Basil Hall, 14
China, 13, 81, 123; defeated by Japan (1895), 27, 32, 37; economic competition of, 146; influences of, on Japan, 13, 25–27, 29, 30, 121; invasion of (1937), 33, 38; Japanese attitudes toward, 48, 49, 137, 148; Japanese influence on, 13, 25; policy of, toward Japan, 49
Chinese, compared with Japanese, 14
Chinese Literature, magazine, 81
Christianity in Japan, 27, 30, 110, 123
Churchill, Sir Winston, 48
Cities: migration to, 12, 22; overcrowding of, 9–11; population gains in, 13; World War II destruction of, 33, *40
Civil code, revision of, 45
Civil wars, 27, 29, 30
Classes. *See* Social classes
Climate, 11, 12
Clothing, 61–62, 80; expenses, 63; kimono as work of art, 91
Codes of behavior and ethics: recent changes in, 77, 78–79, 82–83; Tokugawa, 30, 32, 78
Coleridge, Samuel Taylor, 35
Commerce, evolution of, in Japan, 29
Communism: in Japan, 49, 146; threat of, in Asia, 44, 146
Communist party, 47, 80
Confucianism, 15, 16, 30, 49, 119, 123
Conservative party: economic optimism of, 66; election results for, 47, 48; policies of, 49; supporters of, 48
Constitution, postwar, 33, 44, 45, 46; disarmament clause of, 45–46, 148
Cottage industry, *60, 66, 67
Crafts, 15
Crime, 79, 80
Culture, Japanese: conservatism in, 89–90; development

13–14, 26–27; effect of isolation on, 32, 93; imitation *vs.* originality in, 15–16, 25–27, 89, 105; neglect of rationality in, 16, 77–78

Dan, Reiko, *86
Dance, 92, 93, 109, 110, *114–115
Dating, 82
Dazai, Osamu, 80
De Gaulle, Charles, 48, 146
Defense, 46, 47, 147, 148
Democracy in Japan: beginnings of, 32, 33, 45; postwar, 45, 50–51; U. S. policy toward, 44
Democratic Socialist party, 49
Dewey, John, 135
Diet, *42, 47, 141; postwar elections for, 43, 47, 124; prewar, 33
Disarmament, 44, 45–46
Drama. *See* Theater arts
Dress. *See* Clothing
Duck netting, 108

Earthquakes, 12, 32
East Indies, Japanese trade with, 29
Economic Planning Board, 13
Economic policy, 49
Economy: annual growth of, 64; centers of power of, 66–67; dual structure of, 66, 67, 68; evolution of commercial, 29; foreign trade, 64; future of, 64, 66; in international depression (1930s), 32; 19th Century, 32; postwar attempt at decentralization of, 45, 66–67; strength of, 146; U. S. postwar policies for, 44, 66
Edo (now Tokyo), 27, 30, 32, 109, 145
Edo Bay, 31
Edo Period. *See* Tokugawa Period
Education, 79; aims and methods of, 135–136; higher, 134–139; literacy rate, 133, 139; postwar system of, 134; prewar system of, 133–134; social studies in, 135, 136, 141; U. S. occupation reforms of, 44, 45, 134–135, 139. *See also* Schools; Universities
Education, Ministry of, 124
Eisenhower, Dwight D., 48
Elections, recent, 43, 47, 48, 49; campaigning for, *52, *54–55, *150–151
Electricity, use of, 10, 12
Electronics industry, 64, *74–75
Emperor: attitudes toward, 31, 33, 46–47, 58; divinity of, 32, 33, 123; gains control of

country (1867), 32; present constitutional role of, 33, 46; role of, in early history, 28, 32
Empire, Japanese, *map* 31. *See also* Expansionism
Enoshima, 73
Enshū, Kobori, 88, 96
Entertainment: of average family, 62, *71, 108–109; geisha, 109; movies, 81, 108–109; television, 81, 106, 107, 108; theater arts, 109–110, *114–115; of urban youth, 80, *82–83; western influences in, 108, 110
Ethics. *See* Codes of behavior and ethics
Europe: comparisons with, 10, 12, 13, 68, 123, 125, 133–134; Japanese trade with, 64
Expansionism, Japanese, *map* 31; 19th Century, 27, 32, 37; 20th Century, 27, 33, *38–39
Exports, 64, 75

Factionalism, 30, 79, 80, 134
Family budget, average, *chart* 62
Family hierarchy, 30, 78; post-World War I criticism of, 32, 45; post-World War II changes in, 45, 78–79, 83
Family life, 16, 63, *69, *71, 78–79, 108
Farm population, 13
Farmers: income of, 64; and land reform, 45; living standard of, 63, 68
Fenollosa, Ernest, 93
Festivals, religious, 121, 124, *125–126
Fillmore, Millard, 31
Finance, public, 64
Fishing industry, *73
Fishing rights reform, 44, 45
Food, of average family, 62–63, *69
Foreign exchange reserves, 64
Foreign policy, 48–49
Foreign trade. *See* Exports; Trade
Foreigners, attitude toward, 14, 137
Forests, 10
Formosa, 13; annexation of, by Japan, 32
Fortune telling, 120
France, 146; artistic influence of, on Japan, 93, 94
Franklin, Benjamin, 123
Fudo, god, *100
Fujiwara, Zosho, *128, 129
Fujiwara family, 27, 28
Funerals, 120

Gardens, *88–89, 90, *95–96
Gautama, Siddhartha, 129
Geisha, 109, *114–115
Geisha houses, 106, 109

Genji, The Tale of, Murasaki, 90–91, 107
Germany, 13, 134; Western, economic comparison with, 64
Gluck, Christoph Willibald, 110
Gounod, Charles François, 110
Government: by civil regents, 28; first centralization of, 26, 27; parliamentary, introduction of, 32; postwar, 48, 49; 17th Century centralization of, 30; by shoguns (military dictators), 28–30
Grant, Ulysses S., 94
Graphic arts, 92, 93
Great Britain, 13, 32, 134
Gross national product, 64

Haiku, poetic form, 91, 92
Hankow, China, 38
Harris, Townsend, 36
Hasegawa, Akio, and family, *70–71
Hawaiian Islands, 94
Hayama, Peggy, 110
Health and Welfare, Ministry of. *See* Welfare, Ministry of
Hearn, Lafcadio, 17
Heian-kyo. *See* Kyoto
Heian Period, 27–28, 29, 107; art of, 27, 92; literature of, 27, 90–91
Heine, Wilhelm, 36
Hideyoshi. *See* Toyotomi, Hideyoshi
Hirao, Masaaki, *76
Hirohito, Emperor, 27, 33, *42, 46, *51, 58
Hiroshima, *41, 54; atom bomb destruction of, *40
Homes, 15
Housing: of average family, 63; shortage of, 64

Ibsen, Henrik, 94
Iemoto, 109–110
Ieyasu. *See* Tokugawa, Ieyasu
Ikeda, Hayato, *52–53
Imperial court: in early history, 26, 27, 28; pre-World War II, 33
Imperial palace, Tokyo, 10, *58
Imperialism. *See* Expansionism
Income, national: distribution of, 64; expected growth of, 66; growth of, 64
Income, personal, 64; middle class, 62; working class, 67
India, 13, 33, 121, 124
Industry, 64, *map* 65, 66–67, *74–75; dual structure of, 66; modern plants in, 66, 67; postwar attempt at decentralization of, 66–67; traditional cottage, *60, 66, 67; working conditions in, 67; workmanship in, 64, 74
Insularity, aspects of, 13–14, 32, 34–35
Intelligentsia, political leanings of, 48, 49, 146, 147

Inter-Parliamentary Union, 16
International Organization of Journalists, 138
International payments, balance of, 64
Invasion attempts, Mongol, 27, *34–35
Isolation, period of, 26, 29, 30; effect of, on art and literature, 32, 93
Iwanami Publishing Company, 137, 138, 146

Japan: emerges as centralized state, 30; geography of, 11, 13; geology of, 11, 12; historical periods of, *chart* 27; origin of name of, 10; size of, 13
Japan Congress of Journalists, 138
Japan Teachers' Union, 135–136
Japanese Empire, *map* 31. *See also* Expansionism
Java, 13
Journalism, 136–138
Journalists, International Organization of, 138
Journalists, Japan Congress of, 138
Judō, 112
Juvenile delinquency, 80

Kabuki, 93, 94, *116
Kagesuke, General, 34
Kamakura, 27, 28
Kamakura Period, 27, 28
Kanazawa, 90
Kannon, deity, 130
Kanto Plain, 11
Karate, 108
Karatsu, 127
Karōji, Kentarō, *85
Katsura Imperial Garden, Kyoto, *88–89
Kawabata, Yasunari, 94, 109
Kemari, 107–108
Kido, Takayoshi, 109
Kimono, as work of art, 91
Kinki Plain, 11
Kishi, Nobusuke, 45, 47, 48
Kobe, 11, 13
Korea, 10, 13, 26, 121; annexation of, by Japan, 32; Japanese invasions of, 26, 27, 29
Korea, Strait of, 13
Korean War, 44, 146
Koreans, compared with Japanese, 14
Kosuge toy factory, *74
Kublai Khan, 34–35
Kure shipyard, *72
Kyōdo News Service, 138
Kyoto, 11, 13, 33, 90, 122; geisha of, 109, *114–115; historical mentions of, 26, 27, 28–29, 30, 32; mentioned, 61, 119; old gardens in, *88–89, *95–96; University of, 134
Kyushu, 13

Labor, cheap, 64, 66, 67
Labor movement, 44, 45, 49, 66, 67, 124, 147; Sōhyo, 137–138; Zenrō, 138
Land reform, postwar, 44, 45
Landscape, 11–12
Language, 14, 26; modern influences on, 79; pronunciation of, 15; written, 10
Law: first codification of, 27; postwar changes in, 44, 45
Leisure, use of, 111; of average family, 62, *71, 108–109; reading, 133, 136; travel, 11, 81, 108. *See also* Entertainment; Sports
Literacy rate, 133, 139
Literature, 89, 90; effect of isolation on, 32, 93; of Heian Period, 27, 90–91; modern, 16, 79, 94; poetry, 90, 91, 93; prose, 90–91, 94; of 17th Century, 90, 91; of Tokugawa Period, 78; western influences on, 94
Living standards: of average middle-class family, 61–63; contrasts in, 68; of farmers, 63; of working class, 67
London, 90

MacArthur, General Douglas, 33, 43, 44–45, 48, 124
Magazines, 136, 137
Mainichi, newspaper, 138
Manchuria, invasion of, 33, 38
Manila, 29
Manufacturing, cheap *vs.* quality goods in, 64, 74
Mao Tse-tung, 81
Markets, foreign, 64
Maruyama, Nagasaki, 109
Marx, Karl, 78
Marxist influences in Japan, 32, 45, 48, 49, 67, 124, 137, 147
Matsuoko, Yōko, 81
Medical care, cost of, 62
Meiji, Emperor, 27, 32, 33, *37, 78, 94
Meiji Period, 27, 32, 33, 108; arts during, 93–94, 110
Meiji Restoration, 32, 33, 77, 78, 109
Merchant class, Tokugawa, 30, 109, 145
Michizane. *See* Sugawara, Michizane
Middle class: income of, 62, 64; living standard of, 61–63, 68
Militarism, Japanese, 33, 45, 49. *See also* Expansionism
Minamoto, Yoritomo, *24, 27, 28
Minamoto, Yoshitsune, 28
Minamoto family, 28
Miroku, god, *102
Mitsui holding company, 67
Monasteries, Zen, 124
Mongol invasion attempts, 27, *34–35
Monsoons, 11, 12

Motion pictures, 81, 108–109
Mount Fuji, 11
Mount Hiei, 30
Murasaki, Lady, 91
Muromachi Period, 27, 28, 29, 123
Music, 92, 109, 110; western influences on, 76, 110
Myōhōji Temple, Tokyo, *125

Nagai, Frank, 110
Nagai, Kafū, 109
Nagasaki, 30, 31–32, 109
Nagoya, 11, 13, 29
Nakayama, Miki, 124
Naoshima, 129
Nara, 26, 27
Nara Period, 26, 27, 28
Narihira, 106
Nasser, Gamal Abdel, 147
National income. *See* Income
National Railways, 11, 81, 108, 136, 137; baseball team of, 107
Nationalism, Japanese, 44, 45, 49. *See also* Expansionism
Nature: art inspired by, 89, 91, 95, *98; Japanese sensitivity to, 12, 89–90, 121
Netherlands, the, 13, 31
Neutralism, Japanese, 145, 148; policy of Socialists, 48, 147; promoted by China and Soviet Union, 49
New York, 10, 90
New York Times, The, 46
Newspaper Publishers' Association, 138
Newspaper Workers, Federation of, 137
Newspapers, 133, 137–138
Nihon, 10
Nijō Castle, Kyoto, 29
Nō plays, 27, 92, 94
Nobi Plain, 11
Nobunaga. *See* Oda, Nobunaga
Norman, E. H., 78, 81

Occupation, U. S. postwar, 43–47; Education Mission of, 135; initial policy of, 44, 66; policy shift in, 44, 66; reforms of, 44, 45–46, 134, 135, 139; shortcomings of, 44–45, 135
Oda, Nobunaga, 29, 30
Oeshiki festival, 125
Okinawa, 33, 108
Ooka, 79
Opera, 110; Nō play compared to, 92
Osaka, 11, 12, 13, 90, 105, 106; historical mentions of, 26, 30, 109
Osaka Tigers, 107
Outline of a Teacher's Ethics, An, 135–136

Pacific Ocean, 12
Painting, 89, *98–101; effect of isolation on, 93; of Heian Period, 92; of Middle Ages,

92; western influences on, 93; *Yamato-e*, 92

Pakistan, 119

Parliament, representative, 32. *See also* Diet

Parties, political: election results for, 47, 48; policy differences between, 48–49. *See also* Communist party; Conservative party; Democratic Socialist party; Socialist party

Pearl Harbor, 33

People, Japanese: attitude of, toward foreigners, 14, 137; character of, 14–15, 16, 48, 49, 81; contradictions in, 15–16, 49; imitative capacity *vs.* originality of, 15, 105; origin of, 14, 27; physical appearance of, 14

Perry, Matthew, 27, 31–32, 35, 93; landing of, in Japan, *36

Philippines: Japanese settlements in, 29; Japanese trade with, 29; in World War II, 33

Poetry, 90, 91, 93

Politics, 47–48, 51, 146

Polo, Marco, 10

Population statistics, 13

Prices, 62

Primogeniture, 45, 78

Prostitution, 109

Proust, Marcel, 91

Publishing industry, 133, 136–138

Puppet plays, 93, *117

Radio, 106, 108

Railways. *See* National Railways

Rashōmon, 109

Religion, 119–124. *See also* Buddhism; Christianity; Confucianism; Shinto; Zen Buddhism

Religious sects, 124

Remembrance of Things Past, Proust, 91

Renovationists, 49; defined, 47; election results for, 47, 48. *See also* Communist party; Socialist party

Representatives, House of, 47, 48. *See also* Diet

Restoration, Meiji (1867–1868), 32, 33, 77, 78, 109

Rice: cultivation of, 11, 12, *68; staple food, 62–63, 68

Rinzai sect, 118

Riots, anti-U.S. (1960), 16, 47–48, 80, 138, *144

Rome, ancient, 25

Royall, Kenneth, 44, 46

Rural Japan, 11–12, *22–23

Russia, 27, 31, 32. *See also* Soviet Union

Russo-Japanese War, 27, 32, 33

Ryukyu Islands, 28

Saidaiji, 130

St. Francis Xavier, 27, 30, 68

Samurai, 30; movies, 109

San Francisco Giants, 107

San Francisco Treaty, 47

Sansom, Sir George, 14

Schools: modern school building, *132; work and activities in, *139–141. *See also* Education

Sculpture, *97, *102–103

Seaweed, cultivation of, 12

Sects, religious, 124

Secularization, 123–124

Security Treaty with U. S., 47, 48–49; opposition against, 16, 47–48, 49, 57, 80, 138, *144

Sekai, magazine, 137

Seoul, 10

Sex, 79, 80, 81

Shimabara, Kyoto, 109

Shimbun Rōren, 137–138

Shimmachi, Osaka, 109

Shimoda, 36

Shimizu, Takeo, *85

Shino, Kōichirō, *85

Shinto, 102, 106, 119; and Buddhism, 119, 123; ceremonies and festivals of, 119–120; 124; deities of, *102, 123; essence of, 121, 123; history of, 123; shrines, *map* 122, *127

Shipbuilding, *72

Shoeki, Ando, 78

Shoguns, 28–30, 32

Shōtoku, Prince, 26

Showa Period, 27

Shrines, religious, *map* 122, *127

Siam, 29

Skiing, 111

Social classes: farmers, 45, 63; middle class, 61–63; during Tokugawa administration, 30, 109; working class, 66, 67

Social relationships, 16, 30, 78; recent changes in, 45, 78–79, 82–83

Socialist party, 47, 57; economic views of, 66; policies of, 48–49, 147; speculations on future course of, 147; split of (1959), 49; supporters of, 48, 49

Sōhyō labor federation, 137–138

Sōkagakkai sect, 124

Sony factory, Tokyo, *74–75

Southeast Asia: Japanese conquest of, in World War II, *map* 31, 33; Japanese economic invasion of, 29

Soviet Union, 13; Japanese attitudes toward, 48, 49, 137, 148; policy of, toward Japan, 49

Spain, 119

Sports, 105, 111, *112; baseball, 105, 107; imported, 107; spectator, 108, 111; *sumō*, 105–107, *113; traditional, 107–108

Sugawara, Michizane, 26

Suicide, 79–80

Sumida River, 90

Sumō, 105–107, *113

Sumō teahouses, 106

Suruga Bay, 11

Suwa, Lake, 68

Sweden, 133

Switzerland, 13

Taira family, 28

Taisho Period, 27

Takesaki, Suyenaga, 34

Tanikawa, Kazuho, *54–55

Tanizaki, 15

Tea ceremony, 27, 92

Teachers, 135–136; shortage of, 139

Teachers' Union, 135–136

Technology, 16

Television, 81, 106, 107, 108; ownership of sets, 63

Theater arts, Japanese, 89, 109–110; Kabuki, 93, 94, *116; medieval, 92; Nō plays, 92, 94; puppet plays, 93, *117; of 17th Century, 93; of Tokugawa Period, 93; western influences on, 94, 110

Tokugawa, Ieyasu, 21, 27, 30

Tokugawa family, 28

Tokugawa Period, 27, 30–32, 78, 93, 110; end of, 32, 77; heritage of, 30–31, 33, 109; religion during, 30, 123, 124

Tokyo, *8–9, 12, *21, 30, *58, 124; becomes capital, 32; description of, 9–11, 90, 145–146; entertainment in, *20, 80, 94, 106, 110; foreign community of, 137; mentioned, 16, 53, 75, 79, 133, 142, 149; military parade in (1936), *38–39; population of, 9, 13, 32; scale model of, *111; University of, 134. *See also* Edo

Tokyo Bay, 11

Tokyo Giants, 107

Tokyo Real Estate Association, 11

Toyahama, 127

Toyotomi, Hideyoshi, 27, 29, 30

Trade, foreign, 64; beginnings of, 29; resumption of, after isolation, 32

Trade unions. *See* Labor movement

Traffic problems, 10–11

Travel, 11, 81, 108

Typhoons, 12, 100

Unions. *See* Labor movement; Teachers' Union

United Nations, 146

United States, 13; baseball, compared with Japanese, 107; and defense of Japan, 46, 47, 147, 148; influence of Japanese architecture in, 94; Japanese attitudes toward, 44, 49, 147; Japanese cooperation with, 47, 148; Japanese dependence on economy of, 146, 148; Japanese trade with, 64; movies, compared with Japanese, 108–109; occupation policies of, 44, 66, 134–135; opens trade relations with Japan (1853), 31–32; Security Treaty with Japan (1960), 16, 47, 48–49, 57, 80, 138, 145; suggested attitudes and policies of, toward Japan, 147–148; in World War II, 31, 32

Universities, 134; factionalism of, 79; student life in, *142–143

Urbanization, 12, 22, 32, 33

U. S. Education Mission, 135

Valignano, Alexandro, 68

Veblen, Thorstein, 32

Voting rights: for men, 32; for women, 44, 45, 141

Wages. *See* Income, personal

Warrior class, Tokugawa, 30, 145

Wartime leaders, purge of, 44, 45

Weddings, 120

Welfare, Ministry of, 13, 64, 80

Welfare, public, 49, 64

Western influences, 17, 26, 27, 33, 77; on art, 93–94, 110; on education, 134–135; on entertainment, 108, 110; on Japanese society, 78–79; Occupation reforms, 45–46

Women: equal rights for, 45, 139, 140; voting right of, 44, 45, 141

Wood-block print, 93

Working class, 66; income of, 64, 67; living standard of, 67, 68

World War I, 32

World War II, 30, 33, 77; territories seized by Japan during, *map* 31

Wrestling, *sumō*, 105–107

Writers, popular, 136–137

Writing, Japanese system of, 10, 14, 26; and printing problems, 137

Yamaguchi, Otoya, *56

Yamamoto, Fujiko, *87

Yamato province, 27

Yamato-e, 92

Yamazaki, Kōji, 79, 81

Yokohama, 11, 12, 13, 107

Yoritomo. *See* Minamoto, Yoritomo

Yoshida, Shigeru, 48

Yoshitsune. *See* Minamoto, Yoshitsune

Yoshiwara, Edo, 109

Youth, modern influences on, 78–80, *82–83, 86

Zen Buddhism, 92, 124; beginnings of, 27; influence of, on arts, 91, 92; number of followers of, 119; teachings of, 78, 121

Zen monks, *118–119

Zengakuren, 80; leaders, *85

Zenrō labor federation, 138

Printed and bound by R. R. Donnelley & Sons Company
Chicago, Illinois, and Crawfordsville, Indiana
•
Paper by The Mead Corporation, Dayton, Ohio
and Crocker, Burbank Papers Inc., Fitchburg, Mass.

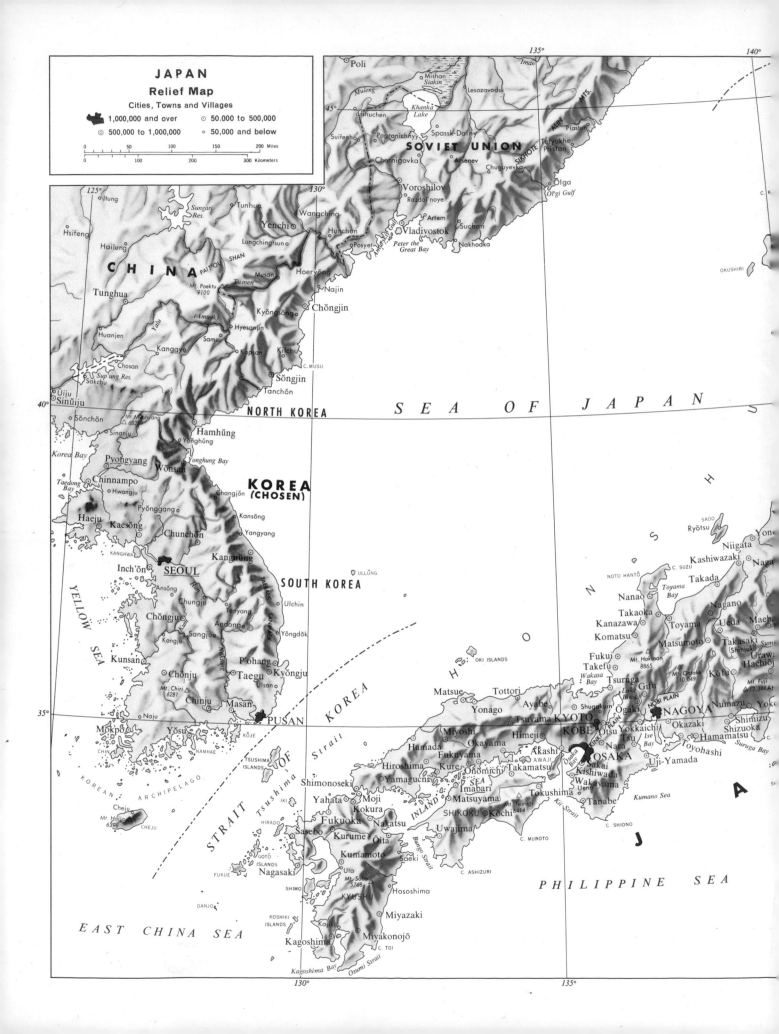

JAPAN
Relief Map
Cities, Towns and Villages

■ 1,000,000 and over   ⊚ 50,000 to 500,000
⊚ 500,000 to 1,000,000   ○ 50,000 and below

0   50   100   150   200 Miles
0   100   200   300 Kilometers

135°   140°

Poli

SOVIET UNION

Mishan
Siakin
Muleng
Lesozavodsk
Iman
45°
Khanka
Lake
Lishuchen
Suifenho
Pogranichnyy
Spassk-Dalny
Chernigovka
Arsenev
Chuguyevka
Voroshilov
Razdol'noye
Artem
Suchan
Vladivostok
Nakhodka
Posyet
Peter the
Great Bay
Olga
Ol'gi Gulf
C. K.

OKUSHIRI

125°
Itung
Tunhua
Wangching
Hsifeng
Hailung
Yenchi
Hunchun
130°
Lungchingtsun
Hoeryŏng
Tunghua
Musan
PAITOU SHAN
Mt. Paektu
9100
Tumen
Huanjen
Najin
(Amnok)
Hyesanjin
Kyŏngsŏng
Chŏngjin
Kanggye
Samsu
Kapsan
Kilchu
Chosan
C. MUSU
Sup'ung Res.
Sakchu
Sŏngjin
Uiju
Sinŭiju
Tanchŏn
40°
Sŏnchŏn
Mt. Myohyang
6820
Sinanju
Hamhŭng

SEA OF JAPAN

S
H

SADO
Ryōtsu
Yon

Korea Bay
Pyongyang
Yŏnghŭng
Yonghung Bay
Wŏnsan
NORTH KOREA
Taedong
Bay
Chinnampo
KOREA
(CHOSEN)
Niigata
Kashiwazaki
Naga
Hwangju
Pyŏnggang
Changjŏn
C. SUZU
N
NOTO HANTŌ
Takada
Haeju
Kaesŏng
Kansŏng
Toyama
Bay
U
Chunchŏn
Kangnŭng
Yangyang
Nanao
Nagano
KANGHWA
Takaoka
Inch'ŏn
SEOUL
Toyama
Ueda
Maeba
Ansŏng
Kanazawa
Ulchin
Komatsu
Matsumoto
Takasaki
Chungju
Shinjuku
Urawa
Chŏngju
Tanyang
Fukui
Hachioj
ULLŬNG
Takefu
Mt. Hakusan
8865
Kōfu
Mt. Fuji
12,388 At
SOUTH KOREA
Andong
Yŏngdŏk
Tsuruga
Gifu
Mt. Ontake
10,049
Kongju
Sangju
Nobi Plain
Numazu
Yoke
Kunsan
Lake
Biwa
NAGOYA
OKI ISLANDS
Shugakuin
Ogaki
Chŏnju
Naktong
P'ohang
Matsue
Tottori
Wakasa
Bay
Ayabe
KYOTO
Okazaki
35°
Mt. Chiri
6281
Taegu
Kyŏngju
Yonago
Tsuyama
KINKI PLAIN
Otsu
Yokkaichi
Tsu
Shimizu
Naju
Ulsan
Himeji
KOBE
Ise
Bay
Hamamatsu
Chinju
Masan
Miyoshi
Okayama
Akashi
OSAKA
Toyohashi
Mokp'o
PUSAN
Hamada
Fukuyama
Kure
Osaka
Bay
Nara
Suruga Bay
Yŏsu
KŌJE
Onomichi
AWAJI
Sakai
Uji-Yamada
KOREA
Hiroshima
Takamatsu
INLAND
Kishiwada
Wakayama
Ueno
TSUSHIMA
ISLANDS
Yamaguchi
SEA
Kii Strait
Kumano Sea
A
Shimonoseki
Imabari
Kumano Sea
NAMHAE
IKI
Yahata
Moji
Matsuyama
SHIKOKU
Kōchi
Tokushima
C. SHIONO
Cheju
KOREAN
ARCHIPELAGO
CHIN
Kokura
SHIKOKU
Mt. Tsurugi
414
J
HIRADO
Fukuoka
Nakatsu
Uwajima
C. MUROTO
Mt. Halla
6398
CHEJU
Kurume
Ōita
Bungo Strait
Sasebo
Saeki
C. ASHIZURI
GOTŌ
ISLANDS
Kumamoto
FUKUE
Uto
Nagasaki
Mt. Sobo
5768
Hososhima
PHILIPPINE SEA
SHIMO
KYUSHU
DANJO
KOSHIKI
ISLANDS
Kajiki
Miyakonojō
Miyazaki
EAST CHINA SEA
Kagoshima
Kagoshima Bay
Osumi Strait
C. TOI

130°   135°